The Little Book

of

AFTER

SPEECHES

The Little Book
of
AFTER DINNER SPEECHES

Edited by

JAMIE STOKES

p

This is a Parragon Publishing Book

This edition published in 2002

Parragon Publishing
Queen Street House
4 Queen Street
Bath BA1 1HE, UK

This book was created by Magpie Books,
an imprint of Constable & Robinson Ltd

Cover illustration courtesy of Photodisc Europe
Cover design Simon Levy

Hardback ISBN 1-40540-211-3
Paperback ISBN 1-40540-137-0

A copy of the British Library Cataloguing-in-Publication Data
is available from the British Library

Printed in China

Contents

Introduction   7

1. I'D JUST LIKE TO SAY A
   FEW WORDS   9
   The fine art of public speaking

2. CONFUCIUS SAY...   29
   Wise and witty remarks and sayings

3. SPEAKING OF WHICH...   107
   A treasury of jokes and humorous stories

4. I THINK IT WAS CHURCHILL
   WHO SAID...   211
   *Retorts, quips and put-downs from the
   great and the good*

Introduction

We all know the scene. Fine Cuban cigar smoke drifts across the table, the chink of crystal as the port is passed to the left and the murmur of intelligent conversation punctuated by an occasional chuckle. The dinner-suited old gentleman says, "Of course that reminds me of a jolly amusing story I once heard at my club . . ." The conversation is hushed as everyone present turns their eyes to the speaker.

If only life were really like that. In reality the idea of speaking before a crowd fills most people with dread, and the scene is more likely to be a village hall than a refined drawing room. Perhaps you know the feeling, a big occasion is coming up and somebody has asked you to "say a few words". Where do you start? Well, this book is here to help. Not only will it give you valuable insights into how to compose a speech that has humour and wit, it also contains a huge archive of humorous stories, witty quotes, wise sayings and other comedic gems.

I'd just like to say a few words . . . deals with the nuts and bolts of putting a speech together. It outlines the dos and don'ts of using comedy in public speaking and gives examples of how seamlessly to blend the comedy resources of this book into your own speech. *Confucius say* . . . is a treasury of those clever little phrases that you hear so often and wish you could remember – prime speech material. In *Speaking of which* . . ., there are a host of long and short stories and jokes that will have any audience roaring with laughter. Many of these are classics, many you may never have heard before. Even if you aren't facing the prospect of making a speech in public, there's plenty here to keep you amused for hours.

In the last chapter of the book, *I think it was Churchill who said* . . . you will find a wealth of aphorisms from some of the greatest wits in history. George Bernard Shaw, Oscar Wilde and, of course, the great Churchill himself are all represented.

Chapter 1

I'D JUST LIKE TO SAY A FEW WORDS

The fine art of public speaking

Fear of Dying

~

There are few things more terrifying to most people than the idea of standing up in front of a crowd of people and delivering a speech. To present yourself for judgement and possible criticism from a group of men and women you may not even know seems to go against every instinct of self-preservation. One survey even recorded that people fear public speaking more than dying! If you only take one thing away from this book it should be this: you are not speaking to a crowd, you are speaking to a group of individuals.

Consider how you yourself feel when listening to somebody give a speech at an occasion like a wedding. Do you sit there intent on finding fault with the speaker? Is your heart full of malice? No, you are there to have a good time and to be entertained. Nine hundred and ninety-nine times out of a thousand every member of your audience will be the same. People don't listen to speeches to find fault with the speaker, people listen to speeches to be entertained and maybe have a few laughs. Most people are as supportive towards a speaker as they can be; half of them are sitting there thinking "thank God it's not me up there".

Even if you take all this on board you are bound to be nervous. Firstly, nerves never killed anybody (with the possible exception of the odd knife thrower's assistant) and, secondly, most professional entertainers insist that nerves are essential to a good performance. There are many actors and comedians who claim that if they ever fail to feel nervous before they step on stage they will retire immediately.

Most of this book is about humour. This is for the simple reason that humour is by far the easiest and most effective way to make a speech enjoyable, both for you and for your audience. OK, if you happen to be Mahatma Gandhi or the Dalai Lama you could probably make a speech without a single laugh in it that would hold people spellbound, but let's be realistic. Make an audience laugh, even a little bit, and they will love you for it. It relieves their tension and provides a tremendous boost to your own confidence. This book will not tell you how to compose every word of a speech, but it will show you how to use humour in a speech effectively.

Writing a Speech

Telling someone how to write a speech is a bit like telling them how to fall asleep – it seems straightforward enough but there is something at the heart of it that you could never get to with words. In the case of speech writing that something is inspiration. There is absolutely nothing you can do to force yourself to be inspired. In fact, the more you try the less likely it is to happen. Like income tax, the best thing to do about inspiration is to ignore it. That's a bit of an exaggeration. What you have to do is engage your unconscious mind on the problem. The unconscious mind is that thing that sits at the back of your brain and comes up with an answer to a problem shortly after you've given up trying to think of one.

Think carefully about the person or thing your speech is going to be about. Think about what you know about that person or thing. Jot down notes of facts, memories, stories or anything that you associate with that person or thing. When you've done all that – go to bed. If it's too early to go to bed, do something else relaxing and engrossing. Whatever you do, don't think about your speech. It's a pretty sure-fire bet that when you wake up, come home from walking the dog or start rewinding the video tape your unconscious mind will slip your brain a note saying, "Hey, what about this for an idea?"

Once the first ideas start to come, the rest will start to flow naturally. As to how you express the ideas, that must be entirely down to you. The way you think, your patterns of speech, your own experiences, in fact everything that makes you an individual among six billion other individuals will all come into play.

Start at the Beginning

~

If you are going to use humour in a speech you might as well start as you mean to go on. Nothing will get an audience on your side faster than a bit of wit. This does not mean that you should stand up and immediately launch into "Doctor, doctor, I feel like a pair of curtains . . ." nor does it mean that you tell them the one about the Rabbi, the Vicar and the Page Three model. OK, this is undeniably humour, but it leaves you nowhere to go. Here are some examples of speech openings that use humour in the right way:

～

Today my boss told me to just relax and be myself. I'm no fool, that's how I lost my last job!

～

This summer I've arranged to go to the Scottish Highlands and take a cottage. My wife said to me, "Surely there are some there already?"

～

Before I begin speaking I'd just like to say that I am absolutely against lewdness, drunkenness or violence. So if you lot could knock it off for twenty minutes and listen to me instead I'd be grateful.

May I say that this evening has gone as well as the host promised it would. He said to me, "This evening will have, flair, pace, humour, style — and then you come on."

∽

I feel I must warn you before I begin that parts of this speech may be unsuitable for people of a nervous disposition. "BOO!" that was one of them.

∽

Here's a snippet of information before we begin. Did you know that it takes more muscles to frown than it does to smile. That's probably why so many of you are smiling now. You're not pleased to see me, you're just lazy.

∽

If you're looking for quality and wit in a speech I'm your man. People have been looking for quality and wit in my speeches for years.

Hello, and thanks for that generous greeting. I've always been a fan of creative sincerity.

∾

Did you know that the human desire for salt has been proven to be as powerful as the human desire for sex. That's why people go to singles bars, it's not to find a partner, it's for the peanuts.

∾

Here's a fascinating statistic. In the 1960s the average number of words in a teenager's vocabulary was 25,000. In the 1970s it was down to 15,000 and in the 1980s it fell to 10,000. Give a few more years and we won't have to listen to them at all.

∾

According to new crime statistics, your car is most likely to be broken into when it's parked in front of your house. From now on I'm parking my car in front of my neighbour's house.

This kind of thing sets the mood immediately and it doesn't leave you stranded. If you know that your audience really appreciates a laugh, and that includes just about everyone on the planet, then you may want to string a few phrases like this together for an opening.

Many of these opening gambits can be adapted depending on your audience or the occasion. Give it a topical slant or mention someone in the room by name.

Middle Ground

~

Once you've won over your audience with a sparkling opening you can move on to the meat of your speech. Of course, what you are going to say will vary enormously depending on the occasion but there are certain rules and guidelines that will stand you in good stead on practically any occasion.

First, and most important: know your audience.

Clearly, a speech delivered at a christening is likely to have a different tone than one delivered at a stag party. You must consider what your audience knows about and what they don't want to hear about. It's no use delivering a cracking line about the frustrations of Windows 2000 to an audience with an average age of seventy-five, it won't mean much to them.

Equally important is to avoid offending anybody. Auntie Gladys may have a mind like a sewer once she's got a few gins inside her, but you can never be sure that you won't step over the line. It's perfectly possible to be amusing without being lewd and this book only contains comedy material that you could safely use on the meekest maiden aunt. Political correctness is a dirty word these days, but you have to admit there is nothing actually wrong with not offending people. For this reason you won't find any racist or nationalistic jokes in this volume either. When it comes to sexism things are not so clear-cut. If you were to censor any remark that made reference to the differences between men and women you would have to cull an awful lot of comedy. For balance, wherever you find a remark about the foibles of women, you won't have far to look to find one about men.

The middle is the part of a speech where there is the greatest scope for the use of humour. This is the place for shaggy dog stories, one-liners or pearls of witty wisdom. The one rule is: keep it relevant. Humour in a speech must arise naturally from the subject or be used to illustrate a point. Avoid sudden wrenches in the flow of your speech just so that you can tell your favourite joke. For example, here is one of the jokes that appear in the section of this book entitled *Speaking of which . . .* :

Two young guys were on holiday in Las Vegas and were having no luck at the tables. Within a week one of them was completely broke. Sitting at the bar, he got chatting to a glamorous older woman who had obviously taken a shine to him. "Listen," he said, "if you could possibly lend me a hundred dollars I'm sure I could win back everything I've lost." The woman agreed and handed over the cash. Within an hour he had lost the lot. Again he begged another hundred off his admirer and again he lost it all within an hour. This went on all night until the guy sat down with his friend and said, "Well, what do you think I should do?" "It's obvious," came the sage reply, "ditch the broad, she's bad luck."

Here's how *not* to include this joke in a speech:

So, I hear the bride and groom are off to Las Vegas for their honeymoon. Have you heard the one about the two young guys on holiday in Las Vegas? Well, there were these two young guys on holiday in Las Vegas and they were having no luck at the tables . . .

This is how it should be done:

So, I hear the bride and groom are off to Las Vegas for their honeymoon. I went to Las Vegas once, back when I was much younger and more handsome than I am today. I went for two weeks with my best friend in those days, Bill Jones. We thought we were going to be high rollers. We'd been there about, oh, four hours before I was broke. I couldn't believe it, so I decided to go to the bar to see if a stiff drink would help . . .

You get the idea. Nobody actually has to believe that the story is true to enjoy it. By telling it as a personal recollection you seamlessly introduce the joke without performing a clumsy verbal U-turn. You'll probably be halfway through the story before your audience even knows that you're telling one. Never announce a joke by using phrases such as "have you heard the one about . . ." or "that reminds me of a funny story . . ." It's corny and it makes a person listening think, "Ah, here's the joke. I wonder if it's any good." Humour should arise naturally and as unexpectedly as possible. Listen to professional comedians and you'll hear them use this trick all the time.

Here's another example. This is the joke . . .

A man bursts into his house one day and shouts to his wife, "Sonia, quick pack your things. I've just won millions on the lottery!" Back comes the excited reply, "Should I pack for the beach or for skiing?" "I don't care where you go," he replies, "just as long as you're out of here within the hour."

. . . and this is a more subtle way of telling it:

Of course, you realize, Bill, that now you're retired you're going to have plenty of time to do the really important

*things in life, such as flossing your teeth . . . or choosing
your lottery numbers. I dreamt I won the lottery the other
day. I rushed home, burst into the house and shouted to
my wife, "Mary, quick pack your things. I've just won
millions on the lottery . . ."*

By the time the audience realizes that it's unlikely
that you included a dream you had "the other day" in
a carefully prepared speech, you're into the punchline
and they don't care.

There are countless ways that you can lead into a
story joke. You can pretend it is something that you
read in a newspaper or a magazine. It could be a story
that a friend told you, or you could pretend that you
heard it from a famous person who you happened to
meet at another function. People are often more
likely to laugh at a joke if they think it comes from
somebody who's known to be witty and clever. The
main things to remember are to make the humour
relevant to what you are talking about, and to avoid
"signposting" humour with hackneyed phrases.

Quotes

A large section of this book is devoted to the wise and witty sayings of famous and respected people (see *I think it was Churchill who said . . .*). These are much simpler to incorporate into a speech than long stories. For one thing you don't have to worry about "disguising" them – part of the point of a quote is that you know who said it. People enjoy hearing the words of people that they expect to be funny and clever. Everybody knows that Churchill was a great orator. If you hear the words "Churchill once said . . ." you're almost laughing before you know what it was that he said. The rule about keeping it relevant still counts though, perhaps even more so. There really is no point in quoting somebody unless you are using the quote to make a point. Here's a simple example of a well-chosen quote in action:

I've known both the bride and groom for many years and I'm certain that they will have a long and happy life together. As Jimmy Hoffa once said, "I have my faults, but being wrong isn't one of them" . . .

Alternatively you can use a quote as an opener. Here's an often quoted story about an exchange between two of the most witty men of the twentieth century put to good use:

George Bernard Shaw once sent two tickets for the opening night of his new play to Winston Churchill. He included a message which read, "Bring a friend, if you have one."

   Churchill replied with a curt telegram, "Regret, cannot attend your play tonight. Will come to second performance, if there is one." I'm happy to be here tonight with so many of my friends, and I hope there will be many performances after this one . . .

Words of Wisdom
~

Making people laugh is great. Making them laugh and making them think you're clever is even better. It's for this very reason that you will find the section entitled *Confucius say . . .* in this book. There are dozens of gems of wisdom here that you can sprinkle liberally throughout your speech. They can be used in any part of a speech, opening, middle or end. Often these phrases can be used effectively as closing comments, as in the often heard words "before I sit down I'd just like to leave you with this thought . . ." This has the advantage of being tried and tested and the disadvantage of being . . . tried and tested – in other words, everybody's heard it. Of course the audience may not have heard the particular thought that you want to leave them with. You will have to judge for yourself whether or not it is appropriate to a particular occasion.

In the End
~

There is only one thing to remember about composing the ending to a speech: it must obviously *be* an ending. There is nothing worse than coming to the end of your speech only to find that your audience doesn't realize. The best you can hope for in that situation is a few moments' awkward silence followed by ragged applause, instead of the riotous standing ovation that you deserve. Just imagine how you would feel if you had read a really absorbing novel only to discover that the last page was missing. Usually, nothing important in terms of the actual story happens on the last page of a novel, but those few closing lines are vital to your enjoyment of the experience over all.

There are many ways that you can let your audience know that you are coming to a conclusion. The most obvious, and safest, is simply to say it. Your last few phrases may begin with something like "In conclusion, I'd just like to say . . ." or "Before I go I'd like to mention . . ." These are clear and obvious signposts to an audience. They are ready for what follows to be your final remark and are already mentally preparing to applaud you.

Quotes and other wise and witty sayings are ideal for closing remarks of this kind. In this case the rule about keeping things relevant doesn't really apply. It's an excepted convention to end a speech with a wise saying that has nothing to do with what you've been talking about, generally the more off-the-wall and amusing it is the better:

I'll leave you with this thought as you enjoy the rest of your meal: wear one watch and you'll always know what time it is. Wear two and you'll never be sure.

Nevertheless there is a lot to be said for keeping things relevant. Among the huge list of witty sayings and quotes in this book you are bound to find at least one that is relevant to your speech, the occasion, a current news story or even to a specific person in the audience who is important to the proceedings. For example, at a wedding:

In conclusion, I'd like to thank Bill Jones for paying for this magnificent spread and leave him with these words of consolation: if money could talk, it would say "goodbye"!

Enough of the preamble. It's time to move on to the meat. In the coming sections you will find enough humorous stories, witty sayings and punchy quotes to keep you going for years. Enjoy them at your leisure.

Chapter 2

CONFUCIUS SAY . . .

Wise and witty remarks and sayings

Snippets of wisdom like these are so compelling because they pull off the trick of combining truth with humour. They are arranged in two sections, those in the first are more light-hearted, while those in the second are more down-to-earth.

～

Lysdexia: a peech imsediment we live to learn with . . .

～

If only women came with pull-down menus and on-line help.

～

Would the Standing Committee please sit down?

～

43.3 per cent of statistics are meaningless!

The difference between tax avoiding and evasion is ten years.

~

Circular Definition: see Definition, Circular.

~

A.A.A.A.A. – An organization for drunks who drive.

~

Madness takes its toll; please have exact change . . .

~

It said 'Insert disk #3', but only two would fit.

~

For a real sponge cake, borrow all the ingredients.

Bacon and eggs: hens are involved but pigs are committed.

~

Which is the non-smoking lifeboat?

~

Originality is the art of concealing your sources.

~

Just fill out one simple form to win a tax audit!

~

Paper clips are the larval stage of coat hangers.

~

Grow your own dope – plant a politician.

Contents may have settled out of court.

~

If idiots could fly, then this would be an airport.

~

A day without sunshine is like night.

~

A seminar on time travel will be held two weeks ago . . .

~

Democracy: four wolves and a lamb voting on lunch.

~

Would you trust a politician to run the country?

~

Improve mail delivery . . . mail the posties their pay.

Treat each day as your last, one day you will be right.

～

Old is always fifteen years older than I am.

～

5 out of 4 people have trouble with fractions.

～

I am the root of some evil . . . send some money.

～

Remember the seven deadly sins, and have a great week.

～

The buck doesn't even slow down here!

Don't assume malice for what stupidity can explain.

~

If you think talk is cheap, try hiring a lawyer.

~

Don't be sexist. Broads hate that.

~

Oh, no! Not another learning experience!

~

The only cure for insomnia is to get more sleep.

~

Don't question authority . . . It hasn't got a clue.

~

Advice is free: the right answer will cost plenty.

He who laughs last is slow.

~

Multitasking: screwing up several things at once.

~

Looking for a helping hand? There's one on your arm.

~

Don't take life too seriously, it's not permanent.

~

Don't insult the crocodile until after you cross the river.

~

The trouble with political jokes is they get elected.

A conclusion is where you got tired of thinking.

~

Nothing's impossible for those who don't have to do it.

~

History is a set of lies agreed upon by the victor.

~

After four decimal places, nobody cares.

~

One good turn gets all the blankets.

~

Almost all loan officers have artificial hearts.

Two can live as cheaply as one, for half as long.

≈

War never decides who is right, only who is left.

≈

A job is nice but it interferes with my life.

≈

"Criminal Lawyer" is a redundancy.

≈

Don't worry: the answer's at the back of the book.

≈

Support the right to arm bears.

≈

We do precision guesswork.

My life has a superb cast, but I can't figure out the plot.

~

Don't let school interfere with your education.

~

A penny saved is a government oversight.

~

Smash forehead on keyboard to continue . . .

~

Shin: device for finding furniture in the dark.

~

Eagles may soar, but weasels don't get sucked into jet engines.

I'm not cheap, but I am on special this week.

~

I drive way too fast to worry about cholesterol.

~

Mind like a steel trap – rusty and illegal in many countries.

~

Support bacteria – they're the only culture some people have.

~

Televangelists: the Pro Wrestlers of religion.

~

The only substitute for good manners is fast reflexes.

When everything's coming your way, you're in the wrong lane.

~

If everything seems to be going well, you have obviously overlooked something.

~

Many people quit looking for work when they find a job.

~

When I'm not in my right mind, my left mind gets pretty crowded.

~

Laughing stock: cattle with a sense of humour.

~

Black holes are where God divided by zero.

I'm a light eater. As soon as it gets light, I start eating.

~

How do you get down off an elephant?
You don't, you get down off a duck.

~

Height of confidence: standing up in a hammock.

~

Make a speech interesting, say: I stand here before
you to look behind you to tell you of something I
know nothing about.

~

A college lecturer is someone who talks in someone
else's sleep.

~

A closed mouth gathers no feet.

Sincerity is the secret of success – if you can fake that you've got it made.

~

You are more likely to get forgiveness than permission, so you might as well go ahead and do it anyway.

~

When in doubt, mumble.

~

Wear one watch and you'll always know what time it is. Wear two and you'll never be sure.

~

Golden rules – whoever has the gold makes the rules.

There are two types of people. Those who divide people into types, and the rest of us.

~

The first 90 per cent of a job takes 90 per cent of the time. The last 10 per cent takes the other 90 per cent.

~

Everybody lies most of the time, but most of the time nobody is listening.

~

If at first you don't succeed . . . so much for skydiving.

~

No matter what you do, there's always someone who just *knew* you would.

You know your children are growing up when they stop asking you where they came from and start refusing to tell you where they are going.

~

Always tell the truth, that way you don't have to remember what you said.

~

If you find a road with no obstacles you'll probably find that it doesn't lead anywhere.

~

Life is a learning experience – the only trouble is, you get the tests before you've learnt the lessons.

~

Future: that period of time in which our affairs prosper, our friends are true and our happiness is assured.

Technology: the knack of so arranging the world that we need not experience it.

~

Autobiography: an obituary in serial form with the last instalment missing.

~

Insider trading: stealing too fast.

~

Gossip: hearing something you like about someone you don't.

~

Egotist: a person more interested in himself than in me.

Diplomacy: the art of letting somebody else have your way.

~

Alcoholic: a man you don't like who drinks as much as you do.

~

Censor: a man who knows more than he thinks you ought to.

~

Gambling: a sure way of getting nothing for something.

~

Cynic: a man who, when he smells flowers, looks around for a coffin.

Revolution: an abrupt change in the form of misgovernment.

~

Secret: what we tell everybody to tell nobody.

~

Contentment: the smother of invention.

~

Success is getting what you want, and happiness is wanting what you get.

~

Never go to a doctor whose office plants have died.

~

Honesty is the best policy, but insanity is a better defence.

Love looks through a telescope; envy through a microscope.

~

Everywhere is within walking distance if you've got the time.

~

The trouble with being punctual is that there is rarely anyone there to appreciate it.

~

Cast your bread upon the waters, but first make sure the tide's coming in.

~

There is only one truly beautiful child in the world, and every mother has it.

If you think you have influence, try telling someone else's dog to sit.

$\sim$

May you be in heaven five minutes before the Devil knows you're dead.

$\sim$

If you want to open a jar with a tight lid, just leave it on the table and tell your children not to touch it.

$\sim$

The secret of immortality dies with me.

$\sim$

Any child will run an errand if you ask at bedtime.

$\sim$

Its easier to suffer in silence if you're positive someone's watching.

Put a FOR SALE sign in your front garden and you'll be amazed at how friendly your neighbours become.

~

Nothing makes a person more productive than the last minute.

~

Life is 10 per cent what you make it, and 90 per cent how you take it.

~

You may be worse off than you were yesterday but at least you're better off than you will be tomorrow.

~

There are no new sins – the old ones just get more publicity today.

Things work out best for those who make the best of the way things work out.

~

You're never as stupid as when you think you know everything.

~

If your ship hasn't come in yet, swim out to it.

~

You don't get ulcers from what you eat. You get ulcers from what's eating you.

~

The only person who never steps on anyone's toes isn't going anywhere.

Tell your boss what you really think of him and the truth will set you free.

~

The quickest way to get into debt is by trying to keep up with people who are already there.

~

The only place you find success before work is in the dictionary.

~

You know you're getting old when you decide to procrastinate but never get round to it.

~

There are two sides to every argument, until you take one of them.

Modern art: if it hangs on a wall it's a painting; if you can walk around it it's a sculpture.

~

Nothing makes an uncomfortable bed more comfortable than the alarm bell ringing.

~

The main difference between a man and a boy is the price of his toys.

~

The only sure way of reducing violence is to kill everybody.

~

Exaggeration: a truth that lost its temper.

~

Identify your friends by their enemies.

A woman who doesn't gossip has no friends to speak of.

～

When you make two people happy, one of them is likely to be you.

～

No one is sicker than the man who is sick on his day off.

～

You can take the day off, but you can't put it back.

～

Only the mediocre are always at their best.

～

Always borrow from a pessimist. He won't expect to get it back.

Noah was an amateur. The *Titanic* was built by experts.

~

To be exactly opposite is also a form of imitation.

~

Don't expect anything original from an echo.

~

Don't pray for a lighter burden. Pray for a stronger back.

~

When in doubt, worry.

~

Love your enemy. It'll confuse the hell out of him.

Success is having your name everywhere — except in the telephone directory.

~

Teenagers are also parent-agers.

~

God made time; man made haste.

~

The world is full of willing people. Half of them are willing to act, and the other half are willing to let them.

~

42.7 per cent of all statistics are made up on the spot.

~

99 per cent of lawyers give the rest a bad name.

If it's tourist season, why can't we shoot them?

~

What's another word for thesaurus?

~

Why do they sterilise the needles for lethal injections?

~

What do they use to ship Styrofoam?

~

Why is abbreviation such a long word?

~

Why is there an expiration date on my sour cream container?

Is it true that cannibals don't eat clowns because they taste funny?

~

Why did kamikaze pilots wear helmets?

~

Why do they call it a TV set when you only get one?

~

What was the best thing before sliced bread?

~

If a book about failures doesn't sell, is it a success?

~

What do you do when you see an endangered animal that eats only endangered plants?

Do hungry crows have ravenous appetites?

~

Is it possible to be totally partial?

~

Would a fly without wings be called a walk?

~

Why do steam irons have a permanent press setting?

~

Can you be a closet claustrophobic?

~

Why do they lock petrol station bathrooms? Are they afraid someone will clean them?

Why do people who know the least know it the loudest?

~

If the funeral procession is at night, do folks drive with their lights off?

~

If a stealth bomber crashes in a forest, will it make a sound?

~

If a turtle doesn't have a shell, is he homeless or naked?

~

When it rains, why don't sheep shrink?

~

Should vegetarians eat animal crackers?

If the cops arrest a mime, do they tell him he has the right to remain silent?

~

If you're cross-eyed and have dyslexia, can you read all right?

Parental Observations
~

A child will not spill on a dirty floor.

~

A young child is a noise with dirt on it.

~

An unbreakable toy is useful for breaking other toys.

Avenge yourself; live long enough to be a problem to your children.

~

If you have trouble getting your children's attention, just sit down and look comfortable.

~

You can learn many things from children . . . like how much patience you have.

~

Summer holidays are a time when parents realise that teachers are grossly underpaid.

~

Parents are so excited about the first steps and words of their children, but then they spend the next 17 years telling them to sit down and shut up.

Useful Phrases

❧

There is nothing more fun than being rude to people, especially if you can do it without that person realizing. Here are some phrases that you can use to insult people while making it sound as if you are being civil and wise. Its best to move on quickly if you use one of these, even the dullest wit will work it out in the end if you don't give it something else to think about.

Thank you. We're all refreshed and challenged by your unique point of view.

❧

I don't know what your problem is, but I'll bet it's hard to pronounce.

❧

I like you. You remind me of when I was young and stupid.

I'm not being rude. You're just insignificant.

～

I will always cherish the initial misconceptions I had about you.

～

Yes, I am an agent of Satan, but my duties are largely ceremonial.

～

How about never? Is never good for you?

～

I'm really easy to get along with once you people learn to worship me.

～

You sound reasonable: Time to up my medication.

I'm out of my mind, but feel free to leave a message.

~

I don't work here. I'm a consultant.

~

I'll try being nicer if you'll try being smarter.

~

It might look like I'm doing nothing, but at the cellular level I'm really quite busy.

~

At least I have a positive attitude about my destructive habits.

You are validating my inherent mistrust of strangers.

~

I see you've set aside this special time to humiliate yourself in public.

Confucius *Really* Say . . .
~

The wisdom of the ancient Chinese philosopher Confucius has long been brought into disrepute by modern wags. Here are some of the best of those cheeky inventions.

. . . a streaker is someone who is unsuited for his work.

~

. . . he who crosses the ocean twice without washing is a dirty double crosser.

. . . man who put head on railroad track to listen for train likely to end up with splitting headache.

≈

. . . man who run behind car get exhausted.

≈

. . . man who sit on tack get point.

≈

. . . a bird in hand makes it hard to blow nose.

≈

. . . those who quote Confucius are fools.

≈

. . . man who sneezes without handkerchief takes matters into his own hands.

. . . man who speaks with forked tongue should not kiss balloons.

~

. . . man who leap off cliff jump to conclusion.

~

. . . even the greatest of whales is helpless in middle of desert.

~

. . . man who drive like hell bound to get there.

~

. . . man with one chopstick go hungry.

~

. . . man who keep feet firmly on ground have trouble putting on trousers.

. . . war not determine who is right, war determine who is left.

~

. . . man who run in front of car get tired.

~

. . . Confucius say too damn much.

~

. . . man who sleep on railroad tracks wake up with split personality.

~

. . . man who live in glass house, dress in basement.

~

. . . man who sit on an upturned drawing pin shall surely rise.

Oxymorons

~

An oxymoron is a phrase in which two words with opposite or contradictory meanings are used together. A classic example would be something like "she's just a poor little rich girl". When you listen carefully to the kinds of things that people say every day you'll be amazed at how often these phrases crop up – usually completely unintentionally. Here's a short list of some of the more common, and bemusing, oxymorons in common use today.

Act naturally

~

Found missing

~

Resident alien

Genuine imitation

~

Airline Food

~

Good grief

~

Same difference

~

Almost exactly

~

Government organization

Alone together

~

Legally drunk

~

Silent scream

~

Living dead

~

Small crowd

~

Business ethics

Soft rock

~

Military intelligence

~

Software documentation

~

New classic

~

Sweet sorrow

~

Child proof

~

"Now, then . . ."

Synthetic natural gas

≈

Passive aggression

≈

Taped live

≈

Clearly misunderstood

≈

Peace force

≈

Extinct life

≈

Temporary tax increase

～ 75 ～

Computer jock

～

Plastic glasses

～

Terribly pleased

～

Computer security

～

Political science

～

Definite maybe

～

Pretty ugly

Diet ice cream

~

Working holiday

Insurance Claims
~

It is notoriously difficult to describe accurately to somebody an event that they didn't see. Insurance companies face this problem all the time. When motorists fill in claim forms they have to include a description of the events that led to the accident. A Canadian newspaper published these extracts from claim forms. Amazingly, these are all absolutely genuine – surely one of the best arguments for wearing a seat belt ever.

I had been shopping for plants all day, and was on my way home. As I reached an intersection, a hedge sprang up, obscuring my vision. I did not see the other car.

I had been driving for forty years when I fell asleep and had an accident.

≈

In my attempt to kill a fly, I drove into a telephone pole.

≈

I pulled away from the side of the road, glanced at my mother-in-law, and headed over the embankment.

≈

The guy was all over the road. I had to swerve a number of times before I hit him.

≈

A pedestrian hit me and went under my car.

I collided with a stationary truck coming the other way.

~

I thought my window was down, but found it was up when I put my hand through it.

~

The other car collided with mine without giving warning of its intentions.

~

Coming home, I drove into the wrong house and collided with a tree I don't have.

~

The telegraph pole was approaching fast. I was attempting to swerve out of its path when it struck my front end.

I was unable to stop in time, and my car crashed into the other vehicle. The driver and passenger then left immediately for a vacation with injuries.

～

I was on the way to the doctor's with rear end trouble when my universal joint gave way, causing me to have an accident.

～

To avoid hitting the bumper of the car in front, I struck the pedestrian.

～

As I approached the intersection, a stop sign appeared in a place where no stop sign had ever appeared before. I was unable to stop in time to avoid the accident.

My car was legally parked as it backed into the other vehicle.

~

An invisible car came out of nowhere, struck my vehicle and vanished.

~

I told the police that I was not injured, but on removing my hat, I found that I had a skull fracture.

~

I was sure the old fellow would never make it to the other side of the roadway when I struck him.

~

The pedestrian had no idea which way to go, so I ran him over.

The indirect cause of this accident was a little guy in a small car with a big mouth.

~

I was thrown from my car as it left the road. I was later found in a ditch by some stray cows.

Chinese Names

~

This is a favourite kid's joke, Chinese people's names can be made to sound like English phrases.

Are you harbouring a fugitive? – Hu Yu Hai Ding

~

See me A.S.A.P. – Kum Hia Nao

~

Stupid Man – Dum Gai

Small Horse – Tai Ni Po Ni

~

Your price is too high! – No Bai Dam Thing!

~

Did you go to the beach? – Wai Yu So Tan

~

I bumped into a coffee table – Ai Bang Mai Ni

~

I think you need a facelift – Chin Tu Fat

~

It's very dark in here – Wai So Dim?

~

Has your flight been delayed? – Hao Long Wei Ting

That was an unauthorized execution – Lin Ching

～

I thought you were on a diet – Wai Yu Mun Ching?

～

This is a clamping zone – No Pah King

～

Do you know lyrics to the Macarena? – Wai Yu Sing
Dum Song

～

You are not very bright – Yu So Dum

～

I got this for free – Ai No Pei

I am not guilty – Wai Hang Mi?

~

Please, stay a while longer – Wai Go Nao?

~

Meeting was scheduled for next week – Wai You Kum Nao

~

They have arrived – Hia Dei Kum

~

Stay out of sight – Lei Lo

~

He's cleaning his automobile – Wa Shing Ka

~

He is a fat man – Wun Fat Gai

Signs You're a Drunk

~

You lose arguments with inanimate objects.

~

You have to hold on to the lawn to keep from falling off the earth.

~

Your job interferes with your drinking.

~

Your doctor finds traces of blood in your alcohol stream.

~

You sincerely believe alcohol to be the elusive fifth food group.

Twenty-four hours in a day, twenty-four beers in a case. Coincidence? I think not!

~

Two hands and just one mouth, now that's a drinking problem!

~

You can focus better with one eye closed.

~

The parking lot seems to have moved while you were in the bar.

~

You fall off the floor.

~

Your twin sons are named Barley and Hops.

Mosquitoes fall over after attacking you.

~

At AA meetings you forget your name.

~

Your idea of cutting back is less salt.

~

The whole bar greets you when you come in.

~

You don't recognize your wife unless you see her through the bottom of a glass.

~

That damned pink elephant followed you home again.

~

"I'm as jober as a sudge."

Dumb and Dumber

～

Nothing gets a laugh like calling someone stupid in a clever way. The technique of gently making fun of someone is well known to professional speakers and comedians. As long as you use these phrases in a good-humoured manner, about a person you can trust not to take it the wrong way, you're bound to get a belly laugh.

For best results you may want to string a few of them together. Once your audience gets the idea you can build up a real head of comedy steam by reeling them off. Something along the lines of: "I've known the groom for many years and, sadly, I have to tell you I've begun to suspect that he's a few feathers short of a duck if you know what I mean. Frankly he's a prime candidate for natural de-selection. I've heard him claim to have a photographic memory – all I can say is that may be true, but apparently the lens cap is glued on . . ."

A few beers short of a six-pack.

A few clowns short of a circus.

~

A few feathers short of a whole duck.

~

A few fries short of a Happy Meal.

~

A few peas short of a casserole.

~

A gross ignoramus: 144 times worse than an ordinary ignoramus.

~

A photographic memory but with the lens cover glued on.

A prime candidate for natural de-selection.

~

A room temperature IQ.

~

All foam, no beer.

~

An experiment in artificial stupidity.

~

An intellect rivalled only by garden tools.

~

As smart as bait.

~

Bright as Helsinki in December.

Chimney's clogged.

~

Couldn't pour water out of a boot with instructions on the heel.

~

Doesn't have all his cornflakes in one box.

~

Doesn't have all his dogs on one leash.

~

Donated his body to science before he was finished with it.

~

Dumber than a box of hair.

Elevator doesn't go all the way to the top floor.

~

Fell out of the family tree.

~

Forgot to pay his brain bill.

~

Gates are down, the lights are flashing, but the train isn't coming.

~

Got into the gene pool while the lifeguard wasn't watching.

~

Has an IQ of two and it takes three to grunt.

Has two brains; one is lost and the other is out looking for it.

～

He fell out of the stupid tree and hit every branch on the way down.

～

He's so dense, light bends around him.

～

Her sewing machine's out of thread.

～

His antenna doesn't pick up all the channels.

～

His belt doesn't go through all the loops.

If brains were taxed, he'd get a rebate.

≈

One-celled organisms out-score him in IQ tests.

≈

Proof that evolution CAN go in reverse.

≈

Receiver is off the hook.

≈

Several nuts short of a full pouch.

≈

Skylight leaks a little.

≈

Slinky's kinked.

Some drink from the fountain of knowledge; he only gargled.

~

Surfing in Switzerland.

~

The cheese slid off the cracker.

~

The wheel's spinning but the hamster's dead.

~

Too much yardage between the goal posts.

~

Warning: objects in mirror are dumber than they appear.

If he had another brain cell it would be lonely.

～

If he were any more stupid, he'd have to be watered twice a week.

～

If you give him a penny for his thoughts, you'd get change.

～

If you stand close enough to him, you can hear the ocean.

Newspaper Headlines
～

These are all genuine headlines from newspapers. Use a selection of them to demonstrate the folly of the media, or perhaps just one disguised as a quote.

Something Went Wrong in Jet Crash, Expert Says

～

Police Begin Campaign to Run Down Jaywalkers

～

Safety Experts Say School Bus Passengers Should Be Belted

～

Drunk Gets Nine Months in Violin Case

～

Survivor of Siamese Twins Joins Parents

～

Farmer Bill Dies in House

Iraqi Head Seeks Arms

～

British Left Waffles on Falkland Islands

～

Lung Cancer in Women Mushrooms

～

Eye Drops Off Shelf

～

Teacher Strikes Idle Kids

～

Reagan Wins on Budget, But More Lies Ahead

～

Squad Helps Dog Bite Victim

Shot Off Woman's Leg Helps Nicklaus to 66

~

Enraged Cow Injures Farmer with Axe

~

Plane Too Close to Ground, Crash Probe Told

~

Miners Refuse to Work after Death

~

Juvenile Court to Try Shooting Defendant

~

Stolen Painting Found by Tree

~

Two Soviet Ships Collide, One Dies

~ 100 ~

Two Sisters Reunited after 18 Years in Checkout Counter

~

Killer Sentenced to Die for Second Time in 10 Years

~

Drunken Drivers Paid $1000 in '84

~

War Dims Hope for Peace

~

If Strike isn't Settled Quickly, It May Last a While

~

Cold Wave Linked to Temperatures

Enfields Couple Slain; Police Suspect Homicide

≈

Red Tape Holds Up New Bridge

≈

Deer Kill 17,000

≈

Typhoon Rips Through Cemetery; Hundreds Dead

≈

Man Struck by Lightning Faces Battery Charge

≈

New Study of Obesity Looks for Larger Test Group

≈

Astronaut Takes Blame for Gas in Spacecraft

Kids Make Nutritious Snacks

~

Chef Throws His Heart into Helping Feed Needy

~

Arson Suspect is Held in Massachusetts Fire

~

British Union Finds Dwarfs in Short Supply

~

Ban On Soliciting Dead in Trotwood

~

Lansing Residents Can Drop Off Trees

~

Local High School Dropouts Cut in Half

New Vaccine May Contain Rabies

~

Man Minus Ear Waives Hearing

~

Deaf College Opens Doors to Hearing

~

Air Head Fired

~

Steals Clock, Faces Time

~

Old School Pillars are Replaced by Alumni

~

Bank Drive-in Window Blocked by Board

Hospitals are Sued by 7 Foot Doctors

≈

Some Pieces of Rock Hudson Sold at Auction

≈

Include your Children when Baking Cookies

Chapter 3

SPEAKING OF WHICH . . .

A treasury of jokes and humorous stories

A bluff old general was inspecting his troops when a messenger rushed across the parade ground and said, "General sir, we just received this message for you from headquarters."

"Well read it out man," bellowed the general.

"But sir, I . . ." stammered the messenger.

"I gave you a direct order soldier. Do as I say!"

"Well all right sir," sighed the young soldier. "The message reads: You are undoubtedly the worst, most incompetent, blundering, lame-brained old fool that I have ever come across in the army. You are not fit to command a troop of boy scouts!"

Quick as a flash the general says, "Well done soldier, have that message decoded immediately."

~

An old preacher who roamed the Wild West on horseback doing his best to spread the word of God was asked by a mine owner to deliver a sermon to his miners. "They are a godless bunch," explained the mine owner, "perhaps you can set them on the straight and narrow." Always ready for a challenge the preacher agreed and set up his soap box. The miners were as surly and roughish a looking bunch of men as the old soldier of God had ever seen, but he persevered. Once his sermon was over the preacher passed his hat around the congregation explaining that donations were his only source of income. The hat made the rounds of the silent crowd and was handed back to the preacher completely empty – not a penny was in it. Seeing this the preacher raised his hands to heaven and cried, "Lord, we thank you for the safe return of this hat from the hands of this congregation."

∽

Grandpa was a keen country sportsman and one day he decided to take his grandson shooting with him. Togged up in all his hunting gear, shotgun broken across his forearm, he proudly led little Jimmy down to the lake side. After waiting patiently for a while a lone duck come into view flying over the lake. "Now watch this Jimmy," says Grandpa. He takes careful aim and fires. The duck flies serenely on. "My boy," says Grandpa, "you are witnessing a miracle. There flies a dead duck."

The grizzled old veteran faced the rows of fresh young faces on the first day of the officer's initiative training course. "Your squad is under heavy attack and the situation seems hopeless. Suddenly one of your men drops his weapon and runs past you heading for safety. The eyes of all your men are on you. What do you do?"

One student calmly replies, "I shout after him 'Well done Atkins, hurry back with that ammunition!'"

~

Having paid his bill, a man is leaving a very expensive London hotel. As he approaches the door a smartly dressed doorman holds it open for him. Just as he passes the doorman, a solid silver ashtray emblazoned with the hotel's crest slips from somewhere under his jacket and crashes to the floor. Without a pause the man spins on his heel and asked angrily, "All right, who threw that?"

~

A prominent lawyer fell in love with a promising young actress and was to be seen in all the best clubs and restaurants with her. Everything went well and, in due course, the lawyer began to think of proposing marriage. Mindful of his professional reputation, however, the lawyer thought it best to do a little checking up on his sweetheart's background. To this end he hired a private investigator, conducting the whole business by phone so as to remain anonymous. After an anxious wait he received the report: "Miss Novak seems to have led an entirely blameless and innocent existence. There is no hint of her ever having been connected with drugs, she has never been in trouble with the police and has never even been accused of promiscuity. The only blot on her otherwise pure white copy book is that, of late, she has been seen in the company of a lawyer of dubious reputation."

$\sim$

A well-known atheist goes to visit a humble country vicar. After exchanging cordial greetings, the atheist notices a beautiful silver and gold model of the Earth and the solar system on the vicar's desk. "That's amazing," said the atheist. "I'd love one of those. Who made it?"

"Oh, nobody made it," replied the vicar. "It just happened."

~

A wealthy man decides to go on safari in Africa and takes his favourite dog along for company. One day, out in the bush, the dog starts chasing a butterfly and gets lost. Realizing he is all alone and lost in the African bush the dog sits down and begins to whimper. Just then he notices a lion creeping through the bushes towards him. "I'm in deep trouble now," thinks the dog. At his feet he sees a pile of bones and an idea occurs to him. Pretending he hasn't seen the lion, the dog settles down to chew a bone and, just as the lion is about to pounce, he says aloud, "Wow! That lion tasted great. I wonder where I could get another one?" The lion's eyes become wide with fear and it slinks off into the bush. Sitting in a tree is a monkey, who sees the whole thing. Figuring he can put his knowledge to good use, the monkey hurries off after the lion and soon catches up with him. In exchange for a guarantee of protection the monkey explains to the lion the trick that the dog has played on him. The lion is furious and, with the triumphant monkey riding on his back, rushes off to find the dog. Once again the dog is fortunate and he sees the unlikely pair approaching. Realizing what has happened, the dog sits with his back to the fast approaching lion and when it is close enough says loudly, "Where *is* that monkey? I sent him off half an hour ago to get me another lion and he's still not back!"

~

The salesman sensed that he was close to clinching the deal and boasted, "Yes sir, this little machine will do half your work for you."
"Great," replied the customer, "I'll take two."

~

The old admiral was showing the cynical politician around his ship. "I run a first-class vessel and my crew is second to none," boasted the admiral, "they are all hand-picked men, each one an expert at his job." They walked onto the bridge and looked out over the deck where a sailor was busy with a mop and bucket. "You see that man down there," continued the admiral, turning to his guest, "he's a typical example. I would trust him with my life." Just then a huge wave broke over the ship and swept the sailor out to sea. "You know that man you said you would trust with your life?" asked the politician. "He's just gone AWOL, and what's more he's stolen your mop."

~

A newly married couple had decided to be responsible and make their wills. Waiting in the solicitor's office they talked to each other in hushed tones. "I'm so glad we decided to do this darling," said the earnest young man. "I want you to know," he continued, "if something ever happened to me, I wouldn't mind if you got married again. The only thing I would ask is that you don't let him wear my clothes." "I understand darling," replied his bright-eyed young wife, "you've no need to worry, they wouldn't fit him anyway."

~

The wise old king traditionally took the best horse in his kingdom every year to be part of his stables. One year there was a problem. The king's courtiers brought two men before him, each one owned a superb young stallion but both claimed that the other man's horse was far better. Knowing that this false modesty was just a way of trying to avoid giving up their prized horses, the king quickly thought of a solution. "To settle which is the best horse there will be a race," he announced. "But surely sire," whispered his chancellor, "each rider will try to lose the race?" "I know," smiled the king, "that's why they will be riding each other's horses."

~

Pepe and Jose had been bitter rivals since they had been knee-high to a grasshopper. When they left the village where they had grown up Pepe went into the church and Jose joined the army. Decades passed and Pepe rose in the church to become a fat and rosy-faced cardinal. Jose meanwhile was promoted through the ranks until he was an equally portly and moustachioed general. One day, completely by chance, the two men were waiting on a train platform together. Pepe noticed Jose in his splendid uniform and went up to him. "Tell me porter, is this the right platform for Barcelona." Without betraying a flicker of recognition Jose glanced at the crimson-clad cleric and replied, "Certainly madam, but do you think you should be travelling in your condition?"

~

Young doctor Phillips glanced out of the window of his study one Sunday morning and noticed Mrs Porter striding up his garden path. Now Mrs Porter was a terrible hypochondriac who wasted hours of the doctor's time every week and he wasn't about to let her ruin his one day off. The doctor rushed upstairs to his bedroom leaving instructions for his wife to entertain the unwelcome guest. After about an hour the doctor tiptoed onto the landing and, hearing nothing from downstairs, shouted to his wife, "Has that appalling old woman gone yet?" Thinking fast, his wife shouted back, "Yes dear, she went ages ago. Mrs Porter is here now."

~

A young sailor who had been away from his fiancée for many months was overjoyed to receive a letter from her. She explained that she was being very good and was saving herself for him alone. As proof she had enclosed a photograph that showed two couples arm in arm and her sitting alone to one side. Full of pride the young sailor showed the photo to his captain. The old sea dog studied it for a minute and said, "That's great son, but doesn't it make you wonder who took the picture?"

~

The elderly Archbishop was making a controversial visit to Las Vegas. His publicity advisers warned him that the trip would be fraught with risks, but the churchman insisted that the gambling capital of the world was exactly the kind of place that the church should be trying to spread its message. After a long flight the Archbishop stepped off the plane and came face to face with a horde of television cameras and newspaper reporters. One eager young news hound thrust a microphone in his face and asked, "Archbishop, what is your opinion of the large number of brothels in this city?" Mindful of the warnings he had received the Archbishop thought carefully and replied tactfully, "Are there any brothels in this city?" The next day he glanced at the newspaper to see this headline "Archbishop's first question: 'Are there any brothels in this city?'"

～

It was 1917 and the great German air ace Baron von Berner had just shot down the English number one, Captain Smythe-Phillips, over German territory. War was different then and the Baron felt it was his duty to visit his honourable enemy in the German field hospital. "Is there anything I can do for you Captain?" he asked the pale Englishman.

"Actually old chap, there is. Tomorrow they are going to amputate my left leg. Would you drop it over dear old Blighty for me?"

The very next day the Baron made the dangerous flight and carried out the request.

A week later, hearing that Smythe-Phillips was no better, he made another visit. This time the Captain said, "This afternoon they are going to amputate my other leg. Could you possibly drop it over England for me?"

A man of honour, the Baron carried out the request the very next day.

Another week passed and the Baron heard that the Englishman had still not recovered, so he visited him once more. Smythe-Phillips was paler than ever and seemed close to death. He whispered to the Baron, "This afternoon they are going to amputate my left arm. I have asked you twice and now I ask you again, could you drop it over dear old England for me?" The Baron rose to his full height and bellowed, "What kind of a fool do you think I am, you are obviously trying to escape piece by piece!"

～

Two young guys were on holiday in Las Vegas and were having no luck at the tables. Within a week one of them was completely broke. Sitting at the bar, he got chatting to a glamorous older woman who had obviously taken a shine to him. "Listen," he said, "if you could possibly lend me a hundred dollars I'm sure I could win back everything I've lost." The woman agreed and handed over the cash. Within an hour he had lost the lot. Again he begged another hundred off his admirer and again he lost it all within an hour. This went on all night until the guy sat down with his friend and said, "Well, what do you think I should do?" "It's obvious," came the sage reply, "ditch the broad, she's bad luck."

~

There was a terrible flood and the preacher was trapped on the roof of his house as the waters rose higher. The preacher was a man of indomitable faith and when two men in a rowing boat came by and offered to rescue him he replied, "No need to bother, I have faith that the Lord will save me." Hours passed and the water rose to the preacher's waist. Another rowing boat passed and again rescue was offered, but the preacher simply said, "I do not need rescue, the Lord my God will save me". Even more time passed and the water continued to rise until it was up to the preacher's neck. A rescue helicopter swooped down and threw him a line but still the preacher was unswerving in his faith. "I thank you my sons but my Father in heaven will deliver me from this flood." After a short while the water rose above the preachers head and he drowned.

When he arrived in heaven the preacher was furious "Lord," he said, "I was sure you would save me! Why did you let me drown?" "I can't understand it," replied God "I sent two boats and a helicopter, didn't you see them?"

A double-glazing salesman strides up the path to a likely looking house. Noticing a small boy playing in the garden, he puts on his best smile and asks, "Hey kid, is your mother at home?" "Yes, she is," comes the reply. The salesman knocks on the door and waits – there is no answer. "I thought you said your mother was at home," he says to the boy. "She is," comes the reply, "but this isn't my house".

~

In the surgery of an expensive, private dentist the patient asks, "Doctor, how much do you charge to remove a tooth?" "Two hundred pounds, sir." "Two hundred pounds for half a minute's work, that's outrageous!" "If sir would prefer, I could remove it very slowly."

~

Jimmy and his wife were walking down the high street one evening window-shopping. Tugging on his arm, she stops outside a jewellery store and purrs, "Oh Jimmy, I'd really love a pair of those diamond earrings, they're so pretty."

"Not a problem," says Jimmy, as he takes a brick out of his pocket, hurls it through the window and grabs the earrings. They make a hasty escape and around the corner come across another jewellery store with a display of rings.

"Oh Jimmy, I'd love one of those diamond rings, please, please, please darling."

Jimmy checks that there's no one around, takes another brick from his pocket and propels it through the window. Again he grabs the loot and they shoot off down the street.

For the third time Jimmy's wife drags him up to a jewellery shop window and begs, "Oh Jimmy, look at that beautiful diamond necklace, wouldn't I look great with that diamond necklace?"

"For heaven's sake woman," groans Jimmy, "do you think I'm made of bricks?"

∾

A man bursts into his house one day and shouts to his wife, "Sonia, quick pack your things. I've just won millions on the lottery!" Back comes the excited reply, "Should I pack for the beach or for skiing?"

"I don't care where you go," he replies, "just as long as you're out of here within the hour."

～

A man is holding his wife's hand tenderly as she lies on her death bed.

"Bernard," she whispers, "I have something I must tell you before I go."

"There's no need to tell me anything my dear, all is forgiven." He replies kindly.

"But Bernard, I simply must tell you, it's been a burden I've carried for too many years," replies his wife, growing weaker by the moment. "I've been unfaithful to you darling . . . I had an affair with your brother. I'm so terribly sorry."

"That's all right my dear," sighs Bernard. "I know all about it."

"You mean, you knew and you never said anything?" says his wife, with tears in her eyes.

"Of course I knew," smiles Bernard, "why do you think I poisoned you?"

Little boy to his father, "Dad, how much does it cost to have children?" "I've no idea son," replies his father, "I'm still paying."

❧

Two cannibals are lying around with swollen bellies surrounded by bones.

"Your wife sure makes a great stew," says the first cannibal.

"She sure does," replies the second cannibal, "but I'm sure going to miss her."

❧

Bob is walking along the beach when he spies a lamp half buried in the sand. Having heard many of these jokes before, Bob decides to pick up the lamp and give it a quick rub. Sure enough, out pops a genie.

"Let me guess," says Bob, "I get three wishes, right?"

"Right", says the genie, "but there's a catch."

"Oh dear," says Bob, "and what's the catch?"

"The catch," says the genie, "is that whatever you wish for, your wife gets double."

"That's not a problem," says Bob "first I would like a hundred million pounds."

"Done," says the genie and there is a hundred million in cash lying at Bob's feet.

"Next," says Bob, "I would like a huge mansion on my own tropical island."

"Done," says the genie and the keys are in Bob's hand.

"Now let me get this straight," says Bob "I have a hundred million and my wife has two hundred million. I have a huge mansion on a tropical island, and my wife has a mansion twice the size."

"You got it," says the genie.

"Now for my third wish," grins Bob, "I would like you to scare me half to death."

~

A newly bereaved widow goes into the office of the local newspaper to place an obituary. As she's very short of money she asks for the minimum size announcement and hands over the message she would like. It reads: "Harold Dead. Funeral Thursday." The editor takes pity on the old woman and points out to her that she could have a few more words for the same money. Thinking carefully, the widow scribbles on the end ". . . Grey suit for sale – worn once."

~

A young actor who has been out of work since leaving drama school finally lands a part in a West End play. Excitedly he phones his dad with the news.

"Dad, Dad, I got this great part," he says, "I play a man who's been married for twenty years."

"That's great, son," says his father, "soon you'll be moving on to the speaking parts."

~

Woman in a clothes shop: "Could I try on that dress in the window?"

Shop assistant: "I'm sorry madam, you'll have to use the changing rooms like everyone else."

~

A drunk staggers into a pub and proclaims in a loud voice, "Landlord, drinks all round and have one for yourself too." The crowd in the pub lets out a cheer, the landlord pours drinks for everyone and then takes a shot himself.

"That'll be seventy-five quid for the round," says the landlord, to which the drunk replies, "Sorry, I don't have a penny on me."

The landlord is more than a little annoyed and he throws the drunk out onto the street.

The next night the drunk is back again and once again he shouts, "Landlord, drinks all round and have one for yourself too." The landlord reasons that no one could be stupid enough to try the same trick twice so he assumes the drunk must have the money to pay this time. He passes out the drinks and has one himself.

"Right," says the landlord, "that'll be sixty-five quid for the round and seventy-five quid that you owe me from yesterday."

"Sorry," slurs the drunk, "I don't have a penny on me."

The landlord is outraged and kicks the drunk out onto the street for a second time. The following day, to the landlord's amazement, the drunk is back again.

"Landlord," he shouts, "drinks all round."

"What, nothing for me?" enquires the landlord sarcastically.

"No way," replies the drunk, "you get mean when you drink."

~

In the theatre the usher notices a guy sprawled across three seats. She asks him to move, but all he does is mumble incoherently, so the usher gets the manager. The manager goes up to the fellow and demands that he leave the theatre. Once again the man just mumbles and rolls his eyes. The manager calls the police and when the officer arrives he strides up to the suspect and demands, "Come along, sir, what is your name?"

"George," the man manages to say.

"Right then George," continues the officer, "where are you from?"

Feebly stretching out his arm and pointing upwards the man replies, "The balcony."

~

A man receives a telephone call from his doctor. "I've some bad news and some very bad news," says the doctor.

"What's the bad news?" asks the man apprehensively.

"I got the results of your tests and it looks like you've only got twenty-four hours to live," says the doctor.

"My God," cries the man, "if that's the bad news, what's the very bad news?"

"I've been trying to reach you since yesterday."

～

The Pope has just arrived in the capital city and urgently needs to get to an important meeting. He calls to his driver, a local guy, "I'm late for a very important meeting, can you not go any faster?" The driver is a law-abiding fellow so he does his best but refuses to exceed the speed limit. The Pope becomes increasingly infuriated at their slow progress and finally says to the driver, "I really am going to be late. Why don't you get in the back seat and I'll do the driving?"

The driver is hesitant but, as a good Catholic, feels that he cannot disobey the Pope and agrees. Soon the Pope is in the driving seat and the car is tearing down the street at high speed. Inevitably, a police car spots the speeding vehicle, gives chase and forces it to pull over. The police officer takes one look through the driver's window and walks away to radio his chief.

"Chief, I think I may have pulled over someone really important," says the officer in a worried tone.

"Who is it," replies the chief in an even more worried tone, "the prime minister, the chief of police, who?"

"I'm not sure," says the officer, "but you should see who he's got driving him around."

~

A police officer finally manages to pull over a car that's been weaving all over the road. Walking up to the driver's window, he says, "I'm going to have to ask you to blow into this breathalyser sir."

"I'm ever so sorry officer," replies the driver meekly, "but I have severe asthma and if I blow into that breathalyser it will bring on an attack."

"Very well," continues the officer, "in that case you will have to provide a blood sample."

"I can't do that either," continues the motorist, "you see I am a haemophiliac and if my skin is punctured in any way I could easily bleed to death."

The policeman is a little perturbed by now but he

goes on, "In that case sir I have to ask you to provide a urine sample."

"I'm terribly sorry officer but I'm afraid I can't do that either. You see I am a diabetic and if I urinate at this time of night my blood sugar level could drop dangerously low and I might have a heart attack."

The policeman is now reaching the end of his tether so he bawls, "Would you mind stepping out of the car and walking along this white line sir?"

"I couldn't possibly officer," replies the driver.

"Why on earth not?" bellows the policeman.

"Well," the driver goes on, "I'm far too drunk."

~

One day at the US-Mexican border a guard spots a man on a bicycle with two suspiciously large and heavy sacks slung across his shoulders. Before he will let the man through, the guard insists on knowing what is in the sacks.

"Only sand, señor," replies the Mexican innocently. The guard doesn't believe that anyone would carry two sacks of sand so he orders the Mexican to empty the sacks. Sure enough they contain only sand. The guard is perplexed but there is no law against importing sand so he lets the Mexican go on his way.

A week later the guard is amazed to see the same Mexican; he is riding a bicycle and again is struggling with two heavy sacks. Now the guard's suspicions are really aroused and he asks the Mexican what is in the sacks.

"Only sand, señor," replies the Mexican mildly. Once again the guard orders the man to empty the sacks and, sure enough, they are full of sand. The guard gets on his hands and knees and sifts through every ounce of sand but he can find nothing. Grudgingly he lets the Mexican go on his way.

This goes on for six weeks. The Mexican turns up at the border on his bicycle with two sacks of sand and the guard wastes hours inspecting every grain and never finding contraband of any kind. On the seventh week the guard is at his wits' end when the Mexican fails to turn up. A couple of days later he is off duty in a bar when he spies the Mexican who has been making his life hell. Going over to him he says, "Listen friend, I know you must have been smuggling something, please tell me what it was and I promise I won't breathe a word of it to anyone."

The Mexican is silent, so the guard implores,

"Please, I cannot sleep at night, it's driving me crazy, what were you smuggling?"

"Bicycles, señor."

~

Bob and Harry were keen hunters. It was the deer hunting season so they hired a helicopter to take them deep into the wilderness. Once they had landed on an isolated hillside and unpacked their gear they instructed the pilot to return to that spot in a week's time to pick them up.

Everything went really well for Bob and Harry and they had a great week hunting in the great outdoors. When the week was over they had shot six hefty stags between them and dragged the carcasses back to the hillside where they had arranged to be picked up. When the helicopter arrived the pilot took one look at the six massive stags and told them that there was no way that his little machine could carry that much weight. Bob and Harry were mortified at the idea of leaving their kills behind and remonstrated with the pilot.

"Look," said Bob, "we were out here last year, we killed six stags then and the helicopter that flew us out was exactly the same as yours."

"Yeah," added Harry, "and as a little incentive maybe this hundred dollars would help change your mind."

The pilot was still reluctant but, hearing that Bob and Harry had managed the same thing the previous year, he pocketed the money and helped load the stags.

The engine whined and the helicopter struggled bravely into the air. Just as it looked as if they might make it over the crest of the valley the pilot lost control of his overburdened aircraft and they smashed into the hillside.

Bob and Harry crawled from the wreckage, stunned but miraculously unhurt.

"That was bad luck," said Bob, "do you have any idea where we are?"

"I think so," replied Harry, "isn't this where we crashed last year?"

~

The wind howled and the snow blustered around the old country mansion. There was a persistent knocking at the door and the gruff old general struggled out of his leather chair, with his gin and tonic, to answer it. Opening the door he was struck by a blast of cold air and there, standing on the doorstep, was a tortoise.

"Please sir, could I possibly come in and warm myself in front of your fire?" said the shivering tortoise.

"Certainly not," bawled the general and booted the unfortunate animal into the dark night with all his might.

One year later, the wind howled and the snow blustered around the old country mansion. There was a persistent knocking at the door and the gruff old general struggled out of his leather chair to answer it. Opening the door, he was struck by a blast of cold air.

"What the hell did you do that for?" said the tortoise.

～

Bob was walking by the canal when he spotted a really small man struggling in the water. Instantly Bob dived in, grabbed the little chap and hauled him to safety.

"Thanks," said the small fellow. "I'm really an elf and I can grant you three wishes for saving my life."

"Great," said Bob, "for my first wish I would like a million quid."

"Done," said the diminutive one, "there is now a million quid in your account."

"Great," said Bob, "for my second wish I want a huge mansion in the country."

"Done," said his small friend, "you now have a huge mansion in the country."

"Great," said Bob, "for my third wish I want a hundred beautiful women at my beck and call."

"Done," said the mini-miracle worker. "By the way could you lend me fifty quid?"

"That's a bit strange," thinks Bob, "but what the hell, I'm a millionaire now so why not." Bob gives the tiny guy fifty quid.

"Bob," asks the alleged elf, "how old are you?"

"Thirty-four," says Bob.

"Thirty-four," sighs the little chap, "and you still believe in elves . . ."

~

A famous jewel thief breaks into a country mansion anticipating rich pickings. As he creeps about looking for a safe he suddenly hears a voice call, "Jesus is watching you!"

The burglar almost has a heart attack on the spot but, after a few moments, he convinces himself that he is hearing things and carries on with his search.

Suddenly the voice comes again, "Jesus is watching you!" This time the thief is convinced and he calls out in terror, "Who said that?" "Gabriel," comes the reply. The burglar is really freaked out now and he begins backing out of the room. Not looking where he is going, he trips over something that crashes to the floor and, at the same time, hears a loud squawk. Taking a risk, he turns on his flashlight to see what he has knocked over. There on the floor is a cage, and inside is a parrot. "Jesus is watching you!" says the parrot.

"You stupid bird," says the thief. "I suppose your name is Gabriel."

"That's right," comes the reply.

"What kind of idiot would name his parrot Gabriel?" wonders the intruder out loud.

"The same idiot that named his Rotweiller Jesus!" says the parrot.

～

A fellow was strolling along the bank of a river one lovely summer's day when he came across a fisherman. "Is this a good river for fish?" he asked casually.

"It must be," said the fisherman. "I can't get any of the beggars to come out."

～

It's cup final day and a huge crowd is shuffling towards Wembley. A funeral procession approaches and one chap stops, removes his hat and stands reverently until it has passed by. "That was a nice gesture," says his mate.

"Well," says the chap philosophically, "she wasn't such a bad wife."

～

The manager of a local football team stood before his dejected players in the dressing room after yet another defeat.

"Don't be downhearted lads," he said jovially, "here's what I want you to do. Every day this week I want the whole squad to go out together for a ten-mile run."

"What good will that do?" asked one grumpy player.

"Well," continued the manager, "by next Saturday you'll all be sixty miles away and I won't have to face this kind of humiliation again!"

Two kids were playing football in the street when the mother of one of them came by. "Where did you get that ball?" she asked suspiciously.

"We found it," came the innocent reply.

"Are you sure it was lost?" asked the mum.

"Oh yes," said the boy, "we saw some other kids looking for it."

~

It was cup final day and the stadium was packed to overflowing. One chap struggled to his seat in the front row, right on the halfway line. Just as the match was about to begin he was amazed to discover that the seat next to him was empty. "That's incredible," he said to old gent on the other side of the empty seat, "I paid a fortune for this seat. What kind of idiot would pay for a seat like that and then not show up for the game!?"

"I paid for that seat," said the fellow. "My wife was going to come with me but she died just a few days ago."

"I'm terribly sorry," said the first man, highly embarrassed. "I'm curious though," he went on, "don't you have any friends or relatives you could have offered it to?"

"Oh I did," replied the elderly fan, "but they all said they would prefer to go to the funeral."

～

An old lady was expecting the gas man to call at nine o'clock. Inevitably nine o'clock came and went and no gas man appeared. Then ten o'clock came and went, then eleven and then twelve – still no gas man. Fed up with waiting, the woman decided to go shopping. Minutes after she had left, the gas man drives up, goes to her front door and rings the door bell. The woman's parrot calls out, "Who is it?" when he hears the bell. Thinking that the parrot is the customer he is supposed to be visiting, the gas man calls out, "It's the gas man," and waits for her to come to the door. Seconds pass and the door remains firmly closed, so the gas man rings the door bell again. Immediately the parrot says, "Who is it?" Now a little frustrated the gas man yells, "It's the gas man," and again waits expectantly for the door to be opened. Time passes and again he is disappointed. For the third time the gas man rings the bell, and, for the third time, the parrot immediately says, "Who is it?" "IT'S THE GAS MAN!" screams the guy at the top of his voice. More time passes and still the door is not opened. The gas man is now furious and is convinced that the woman is deliberately trying to annoy him. He begins hammering on the door with his fist and the parrot says, "Who is it?" Now the gas man flies into a rage and, taking a wrench from his bag, proceeds to smash the door off its hinges and rushes into the hallway. Unfortunately he isn't the fittest of fellows and the exertion brings on a massive heart attack that kills him stone dead.

A while later the old lady returns laden with shopping bags. Walking up the path, she is met with the sight of her front door smashed to pieces and a corpse slumped in the hallway. "Oh my God," she shrieks, "who is it?"

"IT'S THE GAS MAN," squawks the parrot gleefully.

～

A man walks into a pet shop and explains that he wants to buy a nightingale because he has heard that they have the most beautiful song in the world. "I'm sorry sir," says the pet shop owner, "it's actually illegal to own and sell nightingales, but did you know that if you take a canary and drill two small holes in the top of its beak it will sing just like one? I can sell you a canary at a good price and tell you exactly where to drill the holes. It has to be done precisely though, or there's a danger that the bird could drown when it takes a drink."

The guy is highly sceptical and suspects that the pet shop owner may be slightly insane, so he backs carefully out of the shop.

A while later he finds another pet shop, goes inside and explains that he would like to buy a nightingale. "I'm sorry sir," says the pet shop owner, "it's actually illegal to own and sell nightingales, but did you know that if you take a canary and drill two small holes in the top of its beak it will sing just like one? I can sell you a canary at a good price and tell you exactly where to drill the holes. It has to be done precisely though, or there's a danger that the bird could drown when it takes a drink."

The man is extremely surprised but, he figures, there may be something to this mad idea. He agrees to buy a canary and the pet shop owner gives him a little diagram indicating the precise spots that the holes must be drilled. "If you are even a millimetre out," the pet shop owner warns, "the bird will almost certainly drown the first time it takes a drink."

The man goes to a tool shop and explains that he wants a very fine drill bit. "What's it for?" enquires the tool shop owner. Sheepishly the man explains about the canary and the precisely positioned holes. "No problem sir," says the tool shop owner with a wink, "I have the very thing." He reaches under the counter and brings out a fine drill bit that looks perfect for the job. "Mind you get those holes just right," says the tool shop owner, "I hear the bird could drown if you are only a millimetre out." The man pays for the drill bit and goes home.

A few days later the man is back in the pet shop wanting to buy another canary. "What happened," asks the owner, "did you get the holes in the wrong place?"

"I don't know," says the man, "the thing was already dead when I took it out of the vice."

~

A woman is walking past her neighbour's house when she notices her digging a large hole in her garden.

"Just out of idle curiosity," she says, "why are you digging a hole in your garden?"

"My hamster died and I want to bury it, if you must know," came the curt reply.

"That's rather a large hole for a hamster isn't it?" asked the woman.

"Well, yes," said the neighbour, "but it is inside your cat."

~

Two cows were chewing the cud and chatting. "I tell you," said Daisy, "this mad cow disease is really scaring me. They say there have been cases on Dairylea Farm just over the hill."

"It doesn't bother me," opined Ermintrude. "It doesn't affect us geese."

~

A blind man with a guide dog goes into a big store, walks to the middle of the store, picks up the dog by the tail and begins to swing it around his head. Seeing this outrageous behaviour, the manager goes up to the man and says rather curtly, "Excuse me sir, can I help you at all?"

"No thanks," comes the cheery reply, "I'm just looking around."

Two racehorses are chatting in the stable. As usual they get around to boasting about their track records. "Well, as you know, Jeremy," begins one. "I've run twenty races and won fourteen of them." "That's a fair record old chap," replies Jeremy, "but as you know I've run thirty races and won twenty-four of them."

Just then a greyhound passes by "'Scuse me," he says, "I don't like to brag but I've run eighty races and I won sixty-four of them."

There is a stunned silence and then Jeremy says, "Good God, a talking dog!"

～

A top management consultant decided to take a relaxing holiday in the country. One day when he was out walking he noticed a farmer feeding his pigs in a most peculiar way. The farmer would lift a pig up to a nearby apple tree and let the animal eat apples off the tree until it was satisfied, then he moved on to the next pig and carried out the same exercise. After watching this for some time the city slicker cannot resist offering the simpleton some sound time management advice. "I say," he called to the farmer, "don't you realize that's a terribly inefficient way to feed your pigs. Just think how much time could be saved if you shook the apples off the tree and allowed the pigs to eat them off the ground all together."

"Ha," snorted the farmer, "shows what you know about farming. I've never met a pig yet who cared one jot about time wasting."

~

A guy is trying to get into a small town night club but the bouncer won't let him pass. "I'm sorry sir," says the bruiser, "but I can't let you in without a tie."

"I'll be right back," says the guy and dashes off to his car. He searches everywhere but the only thing he can find that vaguely resembles a tie is a pair of jump leads so he knots them around his neck and rushes back to the club.

"I suppose that will have to do," sighs the doorman, "but I'm warning you, don't start anything!"

~

A man walks into a pub and there's a horse behind the bar serving drinks. He stares at the horse in amazement until the horse says, "What's the matter with you, haven't you ever seen a horse serving drinks before?"

"It's not that," says the man, "I just can't believe that the parrot sold up."

$\approx$

A policeman was staking out a pub notorious for drunk drivers. Come closing time he sees a man lurch out of the front door obviously drunk and fumbling in his pocket for car keys. The man falls over twice, and tries his keys in four different cars before finding his own. The policeman watches carefully as the drunk starts up his car and drives gingerly out of the car park. As soon as the car reaches the public highway the policeman races into action and pulls the drunk over. Immediately he orders the guy to take a breathalyser test. The guy in the car fumbles about, asks lots of pointless questions and generally wastes the policeman's time but eventually he blows into the breathalyser. With a smile the policeman glances at the indicator, and is horrified to see that it indicates no alcohol at all!

"I don't understand it, I thought you were as drunk as a skunk!" says the policeman.

"Oh no," says the driver, "I'm just tonight's designated decoy."

～

A man walks into a bar and orders ten straight shots of whisky. He drinks each one down as the barman pours them, until the barman asks, "Are you all right, why are you drinking so fast?"

"You'd drink fast too if you had what I've got," says the man.

"Why, what have you got?" asks the barman.

"About twenty pence."

～

A man is in a pub when he spies three attractive blonde women sitting at the bar. He's had a bit to drink so he goes up to one of them and says, "Would you like to hear a really funny dumb blonde joke?"

"Sure, says the woman, "but first I think there is something you should know. I'm a professional athlete, I can do fifty push-ups in under a minute and I could break you in half like a twig. My *blonde* friend here is a karate black belt, she could take your head off in a second, and my other *blonde* friend trains policewomen in self-defence, she could kick you from here to the middle of next week. Do you still want to tell us your joke?"

The man thinks for a moment and says, "No, not if I'm going to have to explain the punchline *three* times."

~

A woman takes her tortoise to the vet because it's off its food and seems lethargic. The vet examines the animal thoroughly and then shakes his head. "I'm afraid it's bad news Mrs Davis. Your tortoise has acute liver failure and will probably be dead in two days."

The woman is shocked at this totally unexpected diagnosis and demands a second opinion. "Well, if you insist," says the vet and he goes out of the room.

A few minutes later he is back with a distinguished-looking ginger cat. The cat looks the tortoise over, sniffs it and prods it with its paw. "Looks like acute liver failure to me," says the cat. "I'd give it two days to live at the most."

"Thanks," says the vet, "that's what I thought."

The woman is appalled at this bizarre behaviour

and demands that the vet get a proper second opinion.

"Well, if you insist," says the vet and he leaves the room, taking the cat with him. A few minutes later he's back, and he's accompanied by a fine looking chocolate brown Labrador. The dog looks the tortoise over, sniffs it and prods it with its paw. "Liver failure," pronounces the Labrador, "I doubt if it will live two days." "Thanks," says the vet, "exactly what I said."

By now the woman is too dumbfounded to complain so she asks for the bill. "That'll be six hundred pounds," says the vet. "What?" shrieks the woman. "I'm not paying six hundred pounds for this farce!" "Well," says the vet, "it would have been a lot cheaper but you did insist on the cat scan and the lab report."

~

The personnel officer of a large company was interviewing a nervous young man for a junior position. In line with her advanced recruitment skills training she asked some unusual questions.

"If you could have a conversation with someone living or dead, who would you choose?" she asked in conclusion.

The young man thought carefully and finally answered confidently, "Definitely the living one."

~

A vacuum cleaner salesman had fast-talked his way into a woman's house in the remote highlands of Scotland and was about to give a demonstration of the cleaning power of his machine. Before the woman could stop him he tipped a bag full of dirt, ash and rubbish onto her floor and launched into his spiel. "Don't worry madam," he said, "if my machine can't remove every speck of that dirt I'll personally eat it off the floor."

"Shall I get you a spoon?" said the woman. "The electricity comes on again next Thursday."

~

A surgeon, an engineer and a software programmer were sitting in a bar discussing which of them worked in the oldest profession. The surgeon pointed out that if God had made Eve from Adam's rib he must have got hold of Adam's rib somehow and that would require a surgical procedure, so his was clearly the oldest profession. The engineer disagreed and pointed out that, in the Bible, it says that God created order from the chaos and that required engineering, so his was clearly the oldest profession.

"Ah," said the software programmer, "but who do you think created the chaos?"

~

A particularly stern and hated lecturer had very strict rules about the exams he made his students take at the end of every month. One of the rules was that students must stop writing at the moment the examination period expired – to continue for even a second after the bell had sounded meant that you got a zero score. One month the eagle-eyed lecturer noticed that one of his students had continued writing for a few seconds after the end of the exam. When the student walked up to hand in his paper the lecturer said, "Don't bother, you get a zero for writing after the bell had sounded." The student looked at him and said, "Do you know who I am?" "No," replied the professor coldly, "and I don't care if you are the son of the prime minister you still get a zero!" "You mean you really have no idea who I am?" said the student. "No, I do not," said the enraged lecturer, "and what's more I couldn't care less." "Great!" smirked the student as he deftly slipped his paper in with the others on the desk then turned and sprinted out of the hall.

～

A man had just gone through a protracted and very expensive divorce in which he had lost just about everything. To try and cheer himself up he decided to take a holiday and booked himself into a little guest house in a charming country village. One day as he was out walking he spied a quaint-looking antique shop. Thinking he might pick up a souvenir he went into the shop and began looking around. High up on a dusty shelf he saw a beautifully crafted porcelain mouse. He asked to look at it and the shop owner got it down for him and handed it over. It wasn't the sort of thing that he would normally have liked but it was extremely well made and something compelled the man to buy it. "How much?" he asked the shop owner.

"Fifty pounds for the mouse and a hundred pounds for the story that goes with it." The man was slightly taken aback but guessed that the shop keeper was trying to pull a fast one on a clueless tourist. "I'll just take the mouse," he said and handed over the fifty pounds.

Outside, the man looked at the porcelain mouse more closely and noticed for the first time that it had a pair of tiny holes in its snout. Something made him put the mouse to his mouth and blow into the holes and he was rewarded by a beautiful, melodious whistling sound. Just then he noticed three real mice come scooting around the corner. They stopped and stared up at him. "Strange," said the man and began to walk away. Soon he heard a scurrying noise and looked behind him to discover that there was now a small crowd of mice following him down the street. He walked more briskly but the mice kept up with him and he noticed more and more mice emerging from everywhere to join them. The man was beginning to panic now and he started to run, but no matter how hard he tried he couldn't shake off the growing horde of mice that clamoured after him. Finally, exhausted and scared witless, he came to a broad river and he threw the porcelain mouse into the water with all his might. To his enormous relief all the mice that had been following him flung themselves into the river and were drowned.

A while later the man was back in the little antique shop. "So you've come back for the story," said the shop keeper smugly. "No," said the man, "I just wondered if you happened to have any little porcelain lawyers."

～

In the cannibal village a cannibal popped into the local butcher's to get some brains for his dinner. "How much for doctor's brain?" he asks the cannibal. "Doctor's brain is two pounds an ounce," says the cannibal butcher. "That's very reasonable," says the cannibal. "How much is engineer's brain?" "Engineer's brain is three pounds an ounce," says the cannibal butcher. "That's very reasonable," says the cannibal, "how much is lawyer's brain?" "Lawyer's brain is two hundred and fifty pounds an ounce," says the cannibal butcher. "Two hundred and fifty quid an ounce, that's outrageous!" says the cannibal. "Not really," says the cannibal butcher. "Do you have any idea how many lawyers you have to kill to get an ounce of brain?"

A lawyer died and went to heaven. Clearly some mistake had been made, but we'll let that pass. In heaven St Peter was waiting to meet him. He held out his hand and gave the lawyer a big smile. "Congratulations, you've broken the record." "What do you mean?" asked the perplexed lawyer. "The record," continued St Peter, "1,260 years, you've beaten Methuselah." "What on earth are you talking about?" said the lawyer. Now it was St Peter's turn to looked confused. "You are Mr Peter Harold Wilkinson?" he said. "Yes, that's me", said the lawyer. "Well," said St Peter glancing down at his book, "according to our records you have been alive for 1,260 years." "There must be some mistake," said the lawyer, "on my last birthday I was seventy-two years old." "I don't understand it," said St Peter leafing through his book with a frown. Suddenly comprehension flooded across the saint's face. "I see what's happened," he said, "some fool has totalled up your billing hours."

~

After leaving college a young man started up in business for himself. He got a loan and equipped a small office in a good part of town. "Appearance is everything," he told his newly hired secretary. On his first day in business he sat at his polished desk in his smartest suit and waited for an idea to occur to him. Just then his secretary came into the room and announced that there was a gentleman to see him. "Great," thought the young guy, "things are moving already." Remembering his own aphorism, he picked up the phone. As the visitor was shown into his office the young man adopted a businesslike frown and shouted into the receiver, "Tell them I won't sell for less than a hundred thousand." Then he slammed the phone down in a businesslike way and smiled at the visitor. "Good morning, and what can I do for you?" he asked. "It's more what I can do for you," said the caller. "I'm here to connect your phone."

~

Henry was a keen golfer who played the same course every Sunday. One Sunday, for the first time in years, his regular playing partner was ill and it looked as though he wouldn't get a game. Seeing how depressed he was, Henry's wife offered to go along with him even though she didn't play. Henry was dubious at first but, after a bit of thought, realized that it was better than nothing. A short while later they were on the course and Henry was as happy as ever. He was playing a great game and his wife was strolling around with him. On the seventeenth, disaster struck. Henry hooked his tee shot wildly and the ball ended up in front of a groundsman's hut well off the fairway. Henry trudged up to his ball and considered it grimly, the hut completely obstructed his line to the green. Just then his wife noticed that the hut had a door at both ends and suggested that, if the doors were opened, he might be able to play through. Henry brightened immediately. He opened one door and asked his wife to go around and open the other. Sure enough he could clearly see the pin through the hut. Taking out his favourite wood, Henry settled himself to make the shot, it obviously wasn't going to be easy and he wanted to make sure he got it just right. Just as he finally lifted the club to take his swing his wife poked her head around the door at the other end of the hut to see what was taking so long. Henry struck the ball squarely, it hurtled into the hut, hit his wife between the eyes and killed her stone dead.

A few weeks later Henry was back on the course with his regular playing partner. Incredibly, at the seventeenth he hooked his tee shot and the ball ended up in the same spot in front of the groundsman's hut as it had before. "You know what," said Henry's friend, "if you opened both doors of that hut you might be able to play through."

"No way," said Henry, horrified, "the last time I did that I ended up with a six!"

$\sim$

A man was walking along a street in Buenos Aries when he heard screaming. As he rounded a corner he saw a multi-storey block of flats wreathed in smoke with flames bellowing from many of its windows. A crowd of people were standing around shouting and pointing up at the top floor. Looking up, he saw a woman hanging out of a window and screaming for someone to save her baby. The man stepped forward and yelled up to her, "Throw down your baby, I'll catch him." The woman shouted back, "That's insane, you'll drop him and he will be killed. I won't do it." "Listen," shouted the man, "I am the goalkeeper for the Argentinean national team. I've played in every international for the past decade, I've never missed a match and I've never let in a goal. I will catch your baby." The woman was incredulous and she shouted down, "You've never let in one goal?" "No, never," he replied, "they say I am the greatest goalkeeper the world has ever seen. Trust me, I won't drop your baby."

The flames were growing more fierce and the smoke was thicker and blacker than ever. "All right then," called the woman, "I suppose I have no choice." Just as she was about to throw the screaming child down to him there was a massive explosion and the baby was propelled high into the air, spinning wildly. The crowd gasped but the goalkeeper stood as still as a rock, his eyes fixed on the baby spinning through the air high above him. As the kid plummeted towards the pavement half the crowd looked away while the other half couldn't keep their eyes off the terrible scene. The baby was feet from the ground when the goalkeeper suddenly moves with lightning speed. He made an incredible dive across the street, caught the baby in both hands, drew it into his chest, rolled and came to his feet in one fluid movement. After a moment's awed silence the crowd let out a tremendous cheer and rushed towards the hero. The goalkeeper smiled nonchalantly, held the baby out in front of him, and drop-kicked it over a nearby house.

Jack was playing the worst round of golf of his life. He was twenty over par by the ninth hole, he'd lost six balls into the same water hazard, broken two clubs, and practically decimated the rough with his hacking. On the green he was about to make a six-inch putt when his caddy coughed – the ball careered wildly off his putter and rolled into a bunker. Jack became wild with anger, "You are without doubt the worst caddy in the entire world!" he roared. "Come on," said the caddy, "that would be a bit too much of a coincidence wouldn't it?"

~

A keen golfer got to meet the Archbishop of Canterbury at a club dinner and decided to ask him a question. "Tell me archbishop," he began, "is there a golf course in heaven?" "As I'm not a golfer myself," replied the Archbishop, "I'm afraid I can't tell you. But I will ask God and I promise to tell you what he says."

A week later the golfer receives a telephone call early in the morning. Answering, he is astonished to find the Archbishop of Canterbury on the line. "I asked God about the golf course," said the Archbishop, "and he tells me there is a wonderful golf course in heaven. The weather is always perfect and the greens are always immaculate." "That's great," says the golfer, "thanks for phoning to let me know." "There is one other thing I think you should know about the golf course," continued the Archbishop. "Oh, what's that?" asked the golfer. "Apparently you're booked to tee off at five this afternoon."

~

A rich, elderly golfer was playing an appalling round at his exclusive club. By the eighteenth hole he was seventy over par. Seeing a water hazard near the eighteenth green the old fellow joked to his caddy, "The way I'm playing today I'd probably be better off going and drowning myself in that pond!"

The caddy regarded him coolly and said, "Frankly, I doubt if Sir could keep his head down long enough to drown."

~

Jose was notoriously unlucky. Anything that could go wrong for him usually did. One day he was making breakfast when he dropped the piece of bread he had been buttering. Looking down, he was astonished to see that the bread has landed butter-side up — for the first time in his life he had had a lucky break. Jose was deeply moved by this experience and went to talk to the village priest. "Tell me Father," he said hopefully, "does this mean that God has smiled on me and that my luck is going to change?" The priest didn't know how to answer this question but promised to look into it. A while later the priest was in the capital so he went to see the bishop and related the tale of the buttered bread. The bishop didn't know what to say, but he promised to look into it. A while later the bishop was in Rome so he went to see a cardinal and related the story of the buttered bread to him. The cardinal was stumped, but he promised to look into it. A few days later the cardinal was in the Vatican having an audience with the Pope, and, inevitably the story of Jose and the buttered bread was related to the pontiff. "What does it mean your Holiness?" implored the cardinal. "Has God smiled on this Jose?" The Pope thought for a while and then said, "Tell Jose he buttered the wrong side of his bread."

An elderly couple were killed in a plane crash and found themselves in heaven being shown around by St Peter. After seeing many wonders St Peter took them to their new accommodation. "And here is your beachside villa. The swimming pool and tennis courts are round the back and there's a pair of brand-new Mercedes in the garage. Every morning some angels will come round to clean the house and cook your breakfast. For lunch and dinner you can visit any one of our bars or restaurants, where the greatest chefs who ever lived will prepare your meals completely free of charge. The weather is perfect every day, your neighbours are the nicest people you could possibly hope to meet and there is no crime of any kind. I'm sure you'll be very happy here — everybody is." With that St Peter smiled and flew away. "Dammit Ethel," said the old guy, "if you hadn't insisted on all that roughage and low cholesterol spread we could have been here twenty years ago."

❧

Jack was a stage magician who worked on cruise ships. One year he got a job on a ship considered to be one of the best in the world and he realized that it could make or break his career. The first night he did his act and, halfway through, he noticed a parrot perched at the back of the hall that seemed to be staring at him. He put it out of his mind and the show was a great success. The next night, as he stepped out to do his act, he noticed that the parrot was there again. All through the evening the parrot stared at Jack and he couldn't concentrate properly. His performance suffered and the show wasn't as well received as it had been the first night. On the third night, disaster struck. The parrot had apparently been studying him because every time he did a trick the parrot would shout out, "It's up his sleeve," or "It's in his other hand," and completely give the game away. The performance was a disaster and Jack felt awful – he still had to perform for another two weeks before the ship put into port. As Jack stepped out onto the stage on the fourth night there was a terrific explosion deep in the bowels of the ship and the hall became a heaving chaos of screaming people and flying furniture. When Jack came to he was floating on a deserted ocean clinging to a piece of wood. At the other end of the piece of wood was the parrot. The parrot stared at Jack and Jack stared at the parrot. For three days and nights Jack and the parrot drifted in the ocean.

Finally, on the morning of the fourth day the parrot said, "OK, I give up. What did you do with the ship?"

～

Old Bill was a strange fellow and one day he woke up convinced that he was dead. His wife tried to persuade him that he was still very much alive but he clung to the delusion no matter what she said. Bill's children and grandchildren all had a go at convincing the old fellow that he was still in the land of the living but he point-blank refused to believe it. Eventually his family became so concerned that they took him to a psychiatrist. The psychiatrist spent many hours with Bill over many weeks but all his skills were of no avail as the stubborn old gentleman still continued to insist that he was stone dead. After a particularly fruitless session the psychiatrist was ready to give up when an idea struck him. Taking down his medical books, he used them to illustrate the irrefutable scientific fact that dead men don't bleed. After about an hour he said to Bill, "So, do you agree that dead men don't bleed?" "Of course," agreed Bill, "everyone knows that!" "And do you still insist that you are dead?" "For heaven's sake, doc, I've told you enough times, I'm as dead as a dodo." At this the psychiatrist took a pin and jammed it into Bill's thumb. A little trickle of blood leaked out. "So what do you think now!" said the psychiatrist triumphantly. "My God," said Bill, "dead men *do* bleed!"

≈

To the young sailor his captain seemed like a god. He was tall, grizzled and his greying beard was always immaculately trimmed – he was the very picture of what the lad thought a naval captain should be. On top of that the fellow was a war hero and had a row of medals as long as his arm, although he never wore them. The day he arrived on board the young sailor resolved to be just like his captain. He watched the stern old man carefully and tried to emulate him in every way. After a few weeks the young sailor got the job of taking a pot of coffee to the captain every morning. This gave him the chance to observe his hero even more closely. Every morning the sailor would knock on the captain's door and take in his coffee. One thing puzzled him, however, as often as not he would find the captain standing at his desk looking intently at a small slip of paper that he would quickly slip into a drawer. The sailor longed to know what was on that piece of paper but he wouldn't have dared ask and going into the captain's desk drawer without permission was out of the question.

Years passed and the captain eventually retired. The young sailor never forgot the lessons that he had learnt from the grand old man and he rose steadily through the ranks until he too became a captain. He was overjoyed when he was given his first command – it was the very ship he had first served aboard. The day arrived and the new captain boarded his ship. He went down to his cabin, the very cabin where he had brought coffee every morning all those years before, and went in. With a gasp he realized that his captain's old desk was still there. Gingerly he opened the drawer and his eyes fell on a small, yellowing slip of paper. With trembling fingers he picked up the piece of paper and turned it over. There was one neatly typed sentence: "Port is left; starboard is right."

~

Many years ago, a large American shoe company sent two sales representatives out to different parts of the Australian outback to see if they could drum up some business among the Aborigines. Some time later, the company received telegrams from both agents.

The first said, "No business here . . . natives don't wear shoes."

The second one said, "Great opportunity here . . . natives don't wear shoes!"

～

Jack was a fighter pilot in the Pacific during World War II. One day he landed his plane on the heaving deck of an aircraft carrier and, pulling his life jacket over his head, excitedly recounted his adventures.

"What a great mission, Skipper. I shot down six zeroes, sunk a Jap submarine and put a bomb right down the smoke stack of a Jap battleship!"

"Velly good Yankee," came the reply, "but I think you make one velly sirry mistake."

～

An American farmer was visiting his cousin in England, who was also a farmer. The English farmer took the American to the top of a hill and was pointing out the extent of his land. "The boundary starts over there," he explained, "runs along the edge of that wood, over that hill, past the corner of that lake and finishes at the road junction over there."

"That's a nice spread," drawled his cousin, "but you should come and see my farm. If I get in my truck at sunrise and set off to drive around the perimeter of my land I can drive and drive and drive until noon and I still won't get around. After some lunch I can drive and drive and drive until supper time and I still won't make it. After supper I can drive and drive and drive until midnight and then, maybe, I will have made it all the way around."

"Yes," said the Englishman, "I used to have a truck like that too."

～

Bill and Henry went hunting for turkeys. After driving for a while they saw a wood that looked like it might be a prime hunting ground. Pulling up, Bill said to Henry, "You stay here, I'll go over to that farmhouse and see if the farmer minds us hunting on his land." Bill went up to the farmhouse, knocked on the door and explained to the farmer that they wanted to hunt in his wood. "I'll give you permission to hunt on my land," said the farmer, "if you do me a favour first." "That sounds fair," said Bill, "what's the favour?" "You see that big brown cow over in that field," continued the farmer, "I've had her for years but now she's sick and has to be put down. I'm so attached to her that I couldn't possibly do it myself, so if you kill that cow you'll save me a vet's bill and you can hunt on my land to your heart's content." Bill agreed to the deal and set off back to the truck to get his gun. On the way he decided to have a little fun at Henry's expense. "What did he say?" called Henry. "That no good lousy farmer," said Bill, loading his gun, "he said no! Well I'll teach him a lesson. You see that big brown cow over there?" said Bill, raising his rifle. "Yes," said Henry. "Watch this," said Bill as he fired and killed it stone dead. A second later Bill was surprised to hear a second shot ring out behind him and he turned to see Henry lowering his own rifle. "Nice job Bill, I got one of his horses. Let's get out of here!"

～

A man rushed into a chemist's and asked, "Do you have anything to stop hiccups?" Without a word the chemist filled a glass with water and then threw the water in the customer's face. After he had recovered from the shock the man bellowed, "What did you do that for!?" "Well," said the chemist smugly, "you don't have hiccups now do you?" "No," fumed the man, "but my wife still does out in the car."

~

It was grandpa's 90th birthday so his daughter got all her family together and phoned him. When she heard the phone being lifted she gave the signal and everybody burst into a robust rendition of "Happy Birthday to you". They gave it everything they had and when they had finished the woman put the phone to her ear. Silence. Worried she said, "Dad, are you there, are you all right?" "I'm sorry," said an amused voice on the other end, "but I don't have any children. You must have the wrong number." The woman was terribly embarrassed and began to apologize profusely. "It's all right," said the man, "you folks need all the practice you can get!"

~

The English language is full of traps for the unwary foreigner, as Henri discovered when he attended a posh dinner in London. Everything was going fine as he charmed and amused his hosts by telling them about his rural home town and his family. "Of course," he concluded, "my wife is a beautiful and understanding woman but, alas, we have no children." As the dinner guests seemed to be waiting for him to continue, he made the mistake of pressing on into unfamiliar vocabulary. "You see," he explained, "she is unbearable." Noticing the puzzled looks on his audiences faces, he sensed that he had made an error and fumbled for another word. "What I mean to say is that my wife is inconceivable." Puzzled looks were beginning to turn to amusement and Henri floundered ever more deeply into the mire. "That is," he said triumphantly, "she is impregnable!"

~

Old Bill had been driving trucks all his life. One lunchtime he decided to stop at a favourite roadhouse for a beer and a steak sandwich. The owner welcomed him like an old friend and Bill was tucking in to his food in no time.

Outside a gang of Hell's Angels pulled up to the roadhouse in a roaring cloud of dust and exhaust fumes. Laughing and swearing loudly, they piled into the roadhouse and ordered beers. The place was empty except for old Bill and the owner, and the bikers' leader decided to have some fun. With a gesture he gathered his gang around Bill in a menacing circle. Bill continued to chew his sandwich and didn't even look up. The biker chief clicked his fingers and two heavies stepped forward. One of them held the back of old Bill's shirt open while the other poured his beer down Bill's back. Bill continued to chew his sandwich and seemed totally disinterested. The head biker clicked his fingers again and the two heavies kicked Bill's chair from under him and proceeded to stamp him into the floor. Bill didn't make a sound. When the bikers got bored of pummelling him Bill stood up, brushed himself down, paid for his lunch and limped out of the door.

The Hell's Angels leader swaggered over to the bar and remarked to the owner, "That old guy's not much of a man, he didn't even try to fight back."

"No," remarked the owner, looking out of the window, "and he's not much of a truck driver either. He just ran over twelve motorbikes in the yard."

The captain stood on the bridge of his multi-million-pound warship peering grimly into the foggy night. Suddenly he noticed a light dead ahead and leapt into action to avoid a collision. The captain ordered his signals operator to contact the vessel by signal lamp and send this message: "Change your course ten degrees to starboard." Almost immediately the reply came back: "Change *your* course ten degrees to starboard." The captain was indignant and sent another message: "I am a captain. You change *your* course ten degrees to starboard." The reply came back: "I am an able seaman. Change your course ten degrees to starboard." The captain was enraged by this lack of respect and sent another message: "I am a battleship. Change your course ten degrees to starboard immediately." Seconds later the reply arrived: "I am a lighthouse. Change your course ten degrees to starboard any time you feel you need to."

≈

Every weekend old Bill took his grandson to the park to feed the ducks. In the park there was a statue of the Duke of Wellington mounted on his favourite steed. Bill was keen on tradition and he was keen that his grandson should know about this national hero. Every time they passed the statue they would stop and the grandson would wave and say, "Hello Duke of Wellington, how are you today?" For several months this ritual continued, until one day the grandson gave his customary greeting then stood staring suspiciously at the monument. "What is it Jimmy?" asked Bill. "Granddad," began little Jimmy, "who is that man riding on top of the Duke of Wellington?"

∽

Young twin boys Billy and Jimmy were forever getting into trouble. They disrupted class, teased the little girl next door, kicked footballs through windows and chased the neighbourhood cats up trees. One day their mother took them to see the local vicar and explained to him that she was at the end of her tether. "Perhaps you can get them to behave," she implored. The vicar was a kindly fellow and didn't relish the idea of threatening or reprimanding the two young scamps so he decided on a more subtle approach. He reasoned that he would explain to them that God is everywhere and so he sees everything that they do and he is displeased when they misbehave.

Billy and Jimmy were ushered in to the vicar's study and the vicar gestured for them to sit. "Boys," he began in his best sermon voice, "I have a question for you. Where is God?" Billy and Jimmy looked at each other, unsure how to answer. "I say again," said the vicar, "where is God?" There was sheepish silence from the two boys, so for the third time, in a very firm voice, the vicar asked, "WHERE IS GOD?" At this Jimmy jumped up, grabbed his brother's arm and shouted, "Quick, Billy, let's get out of here. God's gone missing and they think we've done it!"

～

Old Bill was big game hunting in the African bush. He had been out all day and hadn't even seen any big game, much less had a chance to shoot it. Suddenly, he heard a rustling behind him and he whirled around with his gun ready. Standing not twenty feet away was a huge and hungry-looking lion staring right at him. Bill lifted his rifle with quivering hands and took careful aim at the beast. He squeezed the trigger. Click. Nothing happened. With his heart in his mouth Bill squeezed the trigger again. Click. Still nothing happened. There was a moment's silence and then Bill tossed his rifle aside and ran for it.

Bill ran faster than he had ever run in his life despite his advanced years, but it seemed that there was nowhere to hide. The harder Bill ran the more the lion seemed to gain on him. Finally Bill screeched to a halt on the edge of a precipice. There was nowhere to go and so Bill dropped to his knees and began praying feverishly, "Oh, Lord," he panted. "I pray that this lion is a good Christian Lion!"

As he still seemed to be in one piece Bill opened his eyes cautiously and looked around. He was amazed to see the lion hunched down on its hind legs with its forepaws pressed together in an attitude of prayer. By straining his ears Bill could just make out what the beast was saying ". . . and for what we are about to receive may the Lord make us truly grateful".

~

A young preacher travelled to Australia in the early days of colonization to bring the word of God to the isolated sheep ranchers. One day at a tiny trading post in the middle of nowhere he had advertised that he would be delivering a sermon and was waiting for his flock to show up. The appointed hour came and went and there was just one dishevelled old man standing and looking expectantly at him. The preacher wondered aloud whether it was worth his while delivering his sermon to just one man.

"I don't know about that Father," said the old man, "but I do know about sheep and I know that if I went to feed my sheep and only one of them showed up I'd be sure to feed that one."

The preacher was inspired and launched into his hour-long sermon. He gave it everything he had, and by the time he had finished, he was red with heat and religious fervour. "So, what do you think about that?" he enquired of the old man. "Well, Father, I don't know much about preaching. But I do know that if I went to feed my sheep and only one of them turned up I sure wouldn't give that one the whole load."

~

A highly successful businesswoman died and went to heaven. As she arrived she saw two men ahead of her meeting St Peter. The first man had been a lawyer and St Peter said to him, "Welcome to heaven, unfortunately there has been a change in the rules and you now have to pass a simple test before I can let you in." "OK," said the lawyer, "what's the test?" "Spell law," said St Peter. "That's easy," said the lawyer, "l-a-w." "Well done," said St Peter, "in you go."

The second man had been an accountant and St Peter said to him, "Welcome to heaven, unfortunately there has been a change in the rules and you now have to pass a simple test before I can let you in." "OK," said the accountant, "what's the test?" "What is five plus five?" said St Peter. "That's easy," said the accountant, "the answer is ten." "Well done," said St Peter, "in you go."

Finally the businesswoman came up to St Peter and he said to her, "Welcome to heaven, unfortunately there has been a change in the rules and you now have to pass a simple test before I can let you in." "Look," said the woman, "I've had it hard all my life. I've had to fight for every promotion just because I'm a woman, I've had to accept lower wages for doing the same job as a man, I've been hassled, abused and condescended to every day of my working life and now I arrive in heaven and even you are going to give me a tough time!" "It's a very simple test," said St Peter. "Oh, very well, get on with it then," sighed the woman. "OK," began St Peter, "what number am I thinking of?"

～

The Americans and Russians at the height of the arms race realized that if they continued in the usual manner they were going to blow up the whole world. One day they sat down and decided to settle the whole dispute with one dog fight. They'd have five years to breed the best fighting dog in the world and whichever side's dog won would be entitled to dominate the world. The losing side would have to lay down its arms. The Russians found the biggest meanest Doberman and Rottweiler bitches in the world and bred them with the biggest meanest Siberian wolves. They selected only the biggest and strongest puppy from each litter, killed his siblings, and gave him all the milk. They used steroids and trainers and after five years came up with the biggest meanest dog the world had ever seen. Its cage needed steel bars that were five inches thick and nobody could get near it. When the day came for the dog fight, the Americans showed up with a strange animal. It was a nine-foot-long Dachshund. Everyone felt sorry for the Americans because they knew there was no way that this dog could possibly last ten seconds with the Russian dog. When the cages were opened up, the Dachshund came out of its cage and slowly waddled over towards the Russian dog. The Russian dog snarled and leapt out of its cage and charged the American Dachshund. But, when it got close enough to bite the Dachshund's neck, the Dachshund opened its mouth and consumed the Russian dog in one bite. There was nothing left at all of the Russian dog. The Russians came up to the Americans shaking their heads in disbelief. "We don't understand how this could have happened. We had our best people working for five years with the meanest Doberman and Rottweiler bitches in the world and the biggest meanest Siberian wolves." "That's nothing," an American replied. "We had our best plastic surgeons working for five years to make an alligator look like a Dachshund."

～

A wife and her husband were having a dinner party for all the major status figures in Rome, Italy. The wife was very excited about this and wanted everything to be perfect. At the very last minute, she realized that she didn't have any snails for this dinner party, so she asked her husband to run down to the beach with the bucket she was handing him to gather some snails. Very grudgingly, he agreed. He took the bucket, walked out the door, down the steps, and out to the beach. As he was collecting the snails, he noticed a couple of his friends strolling alongside the water just a little further down the beach. He kept thinking to himself, "Wouldn't it be great if they had an additional ticket for the soccer game and we could go together to see the national team playing Germany." He went back to gathering the snails. All of a sudden he looked up, and his friends were standing right over him. They got to talking, and sure enough they had an additional ticket to the game and invited him to go to the stadium with them. The game ended at eleven o'clock and by the time they got back to their cars, it was midnight. At that point the man looked at the bucket of snails and exclaimed, "Oh no!!! My wife's dinner party!!!" He grabbed his bucket, drove back to his place, parked in the street, and ran all the way to his apartment. He ran up the stairs of his apartment. He was in such a hurry that when he got to the top of the stairs, he dropped the bucket of snails. There were snails all down the stairs. The door opened just then, with a very angry wife standing in the doorway wondering where he'd been all this time. He looked at the snails all down the steps, then he looked at her, then back at the snails and said, "Come on guys, we're almost there!"

~

Betty and Tim were killed in a car accident on the eve of their wedding. When they reached the pearly gates St Peter met them. They asked if they could still be married in heaven. "Well, let me find out if this is possible. Stay there and I will be right back." Six months passed and finally St Peter returned. "Yes, we can do this for you." The couple replied, "Well, as we have spent so much time together waiting for your answer, we need to know if there is a possibility that we could be divorced if the marriage doesn't work out?" To this St Peter answered, "It took me six months to find a priest up here . . . how long do you think it will take me to find a lawyer!"

~

A rabbi and a priest get into a car accident and it's a bad one. Both cars are totally demolished but amazingly neither cleric is hurt. After they crawl out of their cars the rabbi sees the priest's collar and says, "So you're a priest. I'm a rabbi. Just look at our cars. There's nothing left but we are unhurt. This must be a sign from above. God must have meant that we should meet and be friends and live together in peace the rest of our days." "I agree with you completely," the priest replies. "This must surely be a sign from God". The rabbi continues. "And look at this. Here's another miracle. My car is completely demolished but this bottle of wine didn't break. Surely God wants us to drink this wine and celebrate our good fortune." He then hands the bottle to the priest. The priest agrees, takes a few big swigs and hands the bottle back to the rabbi, who takes it and immediately puts the cap on and hands it back to the priest. The priest asks, "Aren't you having any?" "No," replies the rabbi, "I think I'll wait for the police to arrive."

~

A mangy-looking guy goes into a bar and orders a drink. The bartender says: "No way. I don't think you can pay for it." The guy says, "You're right. I don't have any money, but if I show you something you haven't seen before, will you give me a drink?" The bartender says, "Only if what you show me isn't risqué." "Deal!" says the guy and reaches into his coat pocket and pulls out a hamster. He puts the hamster on the bar and it runs to the end of the bar, climbs down the bar, runs across the room, up the piano, jumps on the keyboard and starts playing Gershwin songs. And the hamster is really good. The bartender says, "You're right. I've never seen anything like that before. That hamster is truly good on the piano." The guy downs the drink and asks the bartender for another. "Money or another miracle, or else no drink," says the bartender. The guy reaches into his coat again and pulls out a frog. He puts the frog on the bar, and the frog starts to sing. He has a marvellous voice and great pitch. A fine singer. A stranger from the other end of the bar runs over to the guy and offers him three hundred dollars for the frog. The guy says, "It's a deal." He takes the three hundred and gives the stranger the frog. The stranger runs out of the bar. The bartender says to the guy, "Are you some kind of nut? You sold a singing frog for three hundred dollars? It must have been worth millions. You must be crazy." "Not so," says the guy. "The hamster is also a ventriloquist."

A woman walked up to a little old man rocking in a chair on his porch. "I couldn't help noticing how happy you look," she said. "What's your secret for a long happy life?" "I smoke three packs of cigarettes a day," he said. "I also drink a case of whisky a week, eat fatty foods, and never exercise!" "That's amazing," the woman said. "How old are you?" He thought for a moment, and replied, "Twenty-six."

～

Tom had this problem of getting up late in the morning and was always late for work. His boss was mad at him and threatened to fire him if he didn't do something about it. So Tom went to his doctor who gave him a pill and told him to take it before he went to bed. Tom slept well and in fact beat the alarm in the morning. He had a leisurely breakfast and drove cheerfully to work. "Boss," he said, "the pill actually worked!" "That's great," said the boss, "but where were you yesterday?"

～

Two guys are walking in the desert. One is carrying a lamp post, the other one has a telephone booth. "Why are you carrying a telephone booth ?" asked a passing stranger. "When the lions come, I put it down, get into it and I'll be safe." "Oh, I see," said the stranger. "And why are you carrying an lamp post ?" "When the lions come, I'll throw it away, so I can run faster."

~

A guy goes to visit his grandmother and he brings his friend with him. While he's talking to his grandmother, his friend starts eating the peanuts on the coffee table, and finishes them off. As they're leaving, his friend says to his grandmother, "Thanks for the peanuts." She says, "Yeah, since I lost my dentures I can only suck the chocolate off 'em."

~

Two guys are out hiking. All of a sudden, a bear starts chasing them. They climb a tree, but the bear starts climbing up the tree after them. The first guy gets his sneakers out of his knapsack and starts putting them on. The second guy says, "What are you doing?" He says, "I figure when the bear gets close to us, we'll jump down and make a run for it." The second guy says, "Are you crazy? You can't outrun a bear". The first guy says, "I don't have to outrun the bear . . . I only have to outrun you."

Corny Jokes

~

Everybody loves a corny joke, even if they won't admit it. You might want to throw one or two of these into a speech. If you can get your audience into the mood to laugh, they'll laugh at just about anything. It's also worth bearing in mind that you could face an audience of adults *and* children. Don't deny the kids the opportunity for a good laugh too. If you can get children laughing the effect is usually irresistible to adults, it gives them an excuse to laugh like children too.

How do crazy people go through the forest?
They take the psycho path.

How do you get holy water?
Boil the hell out of it.

~

What do prisoners use to call each other?
Cell phones.

~

What do you call a boomerang that doesn't work?
A stick.

~

What do you call cheese that isn't yours?
Nacho Cheese.

~

What do you call Santa's helpers?
Subordinate Clauses.

~

What do you call four bull fighters in quicksand?
Quatro sinko.

≈

What do you get from a pampered cow?
Spoiled milk.

≈

What do you get when you cross a snowman with a vampire?
Frostbite.

≈

What has four legs, is big, green, fuzzy, and if it fell out of a tree would kill you?
A pool table.

≈

What is a zebra?
Twenty-six sizes larger than an "A" bra.

What lies at the bottom of the ocean and twitches?
A nervous wreck.

~

Where do you find a dog with no legs?
Right where you left him.

~

Why are there so many Johnsons in the phone book?
They all have phones.

~

Why do bagpipers walk when they play?
They're trying to get away from the noise.

~

A man walks into a doctor's office. He has a cucumber up his nose, a carrot in his left ear and a banana in his right ear. "What's the matter with me?" he asks the doctor. The doctor replies, "You're not eating properly."

Why don't lobsters share?
They're shellfish.

≈

Why do cows wear bells?
Because their horns don't work.

≈

Why did the ref call a penalty during the Leper Hockey game?
Because there was a face off in the corner.

≈

Why did the leper crash his car?
He left his foot on the accelerator.

≈

Why do chicken coops have two doors?
Because if they had four doors they'd be chicken saloons.

What's the definition of mixed emotions?
When you see your mother-in-law backing off a cliff
in your new car.

~

Did you hear about the man who was tap dancing?
He broke his ankle when he fell into the sink.

~

What do you get when you cross a dyslexic agnostic
with an insomniac?
Someone who lies awake at night wondering whether
there is a dog.

~

What happened to the survivors of a collision of a red
ship and a blue ship?
They were marooned.

Why did the belt go to jail?
Because it held up a pair of trousers.

~

Why don't cannibals like to eat clowns?
Because they have a funny taste!

~

What did one wall say to the other?
I'll meet you at the corner!

~

What did one elevator say to the other?
I'm moving up in life!

~

Why can't a bank keep a secret?
Because there are too many tellers!

What would you have discovered if you found bones
on the moon?
The cow didn't make it!

~

Why did the dinosaur cross the road one million
years ago?
Because there were no chickens back then!

~

Why did the bird cross the road?
Because it was stapled to the chicken!

~

When is a door not a door?
When it's a jar!

~

If a skunk wrote a book, which list would it be on?
The top ten smellers!

How can you get four suits for a dollar?
Buy a deck of cards.

~

How do dinosaurs pay their bills?
With Tyrannosaurus cheques.

~

What do you call a dinosaur that smashes everything
in its path?
Tyrannosaurus wrecks.

~

What do you call a dinosaur that wears a cowboy hat
and boots?
Tyrannosaurus Tex.

How do we know the Indians were the first people in North America?
They had reservations.

~

How do you make a hot dog stand?
Steal its chair.

~

How do you make an egg laugh?
Tell it a yolk.

~

How do you prevent a summer cold?
Catch it in the winter!

~

How does a pig go to hospital?
In a hambulance.

If a long dress is evening wear, what is a suit of armour?
Silverware.

~

What bird can lift the most?
A crane.

~

What bone will a dog never eat?
A trombone.

~

What can you hold without ever touching it?
A conversation.

~

What clothes does a house wear?
Address.

What country makes you shiver?
Chile.

~

What did one elevator say to the other?
I think I'm coming down with something!

~

What did one magnet say to the other?
I find you very attractive.

~

What did the mother broom say to the baby broom?
It's time to go to sweep.

~

What did the necktie say to the hat?
You go on ahead. I'll hang around for a while.

What did the rug say to the floor?
Don't move, I've got you covered.

~

What do bees do with their honey?
They cell it.

~

What do you call a calf after it's six months old?
Seven months old.

~

What do you call a guy who's born in London, grows
up in Paris, and then dies in Moscow?
Dead.

~

What do you call a pig that does karate?
A pork chop.

What do you call a song sung in an automobile?
A cartoon.

~

What do you call the best butter on the farm?
A goat.

~

What do you do when your chair breaks?
Call a chairman.

~

What do you get if you cross a chicken with a cement mixer?
A brick layer.

~

What do you get if you cross an elephant and a kangaroo?
Big holes all over Australia.

What do you get if you cross an insect with the Easter rabbit?
Bugs Bunny.

~

What do you get when you cross a stream and a brook?
Wet feet.

~

What do you get when you cross poison ivy with a four-leaf clover?
A rash of good luck.

~

What has six eyes but can't see?
Three blind mice.

~

What has a lot of keys but cannot open any doors?
A piano.

What has one horn and gives milk?
A milk truck.

~

What is the best thing to do if you find a gorilla in your bed?
Sleep somewhere else.

~

What kind of cats like to go bowling?
Alley cats.

~

What kind of eggs does a wicked chicken lay?
Devilled eggs.

~

What kind of ties can't you wear?
Railroad ties.

What lies on its back, one hundred feet in the air?
A dead centipede.

~

What do you call a country where everyone has to drive a red car?
A red car-nation.

~

What do you call a country where everyone has to drive a pink car?
A pink car-nation.

~

What would the country be called if everyone in it lived in their cars?
An in-car-nation.

~

What's grey, eats fish, and lives in Washington, D.C.?
The Presidential Seal.

What's green and loud?
A froghorn.

～

What's round and bad-tempered?
A vicious circle.

～

Why did the doughnut shop close?
The owner got tired of the hole business!

～

Why was Cinderella thrown off the basketball team?
She ran away from the ball.

～

Why were the teacher's eyes crossed?
She couldn't control her pupils.

A schoolgirl runs up to her father. She says, "Daddy, Daddy, I need fifty pounds." He says, "Forty pounds? What do you need thirty pounds for?"

~

Did you hear about the idiot who walked around the world?
He drowned.

~

What's the quietest place in the world?
The complaints department at the parachute packing plant.

~

What do you call a Mancunian in a filing cabinet?
Sorted!

A lady came up to me on the street and pointed at my suede jacket. "You know a cow was murdered for that jacket?" she sneered. I replied in a psychotic tone, "I didn't know there were any witnesses. Now I'll have to kill you too."

~

I love deadlines. I especially like the whooshing sound they make as they go flying by.

~

I went to a bookshop and asked the saleswoman where the Self Help section was. She said if she told me it would defeat the purpose.

~

If you ever see me getting beaten by the police, put down the video camera and come and help me!

If your parents never had children, chances are you won't either.

Chapter 4

I THINK IT WAS CHURCHILL WHO SAID …

Retorts, quips and put-downs from the great and the good

Good quotes are gold dust to the speech writer, so here is a whole sackful of them.

Good taste is better than bad taste, but bad taste is better than no taste at all.

Arnold Bennett

❧

A friend is a person that knows all about you, and still likes you.

Elbert Hubbard

❧

The trouble with being in the rat race is that, even if you win, you're still a rat.

Lily Tomlin

❧

A man who moralizes is usually a hypocrite, and a woman who moralizes is invariably plain.

Oscar Wilde

When everyone is somebody,
Then no one's anybody.

W.S. Gilbert

≈

The opposite of talking isn't listening. The opposite
of talking is waiting.

Fran Lebowitz

≈

A camel is a horse designed by a committee.

Alec Issigonis

≈

There are two things to aim at in this life; first to get
what you want; and, after that, to enjoy it. Only the
wisest of mankind achieve the second.

Logan Pearsall Smith

If you obey all the rules, you miss all the fun.

Katherine Hepburn

≈

When a man wants to murder a tiger he calls it sport;
when a tiger wants to murder him, he calls it ferocity.

George Bernard Shaw

≈

Moral indignation is jealousy with a halo.

H.G. Wells

≈

It's a recession when your neighbour loses his job; it's
a depression when you lose yours.

Harry S. Truman

≈

You must come again when you have less time.

Walter Sickert

Life is a mirror: if you frown at it, it frowns back; if you smile, it returns the greeting.

William Makepeace Thackeray

≈

Friends are God's apology for relations.

Hugh Kingsmill

≈

Never go out to meet trouble. If you will just sit still, nine cases out of ten someone will intercept it before it reaches you.

Calvin Coolidge

≈

If you can keep your head when all those about you are losing theirs, perhaps you do not understand the situation.

Nelson Boswell

Work is the curse of the drinking classes.

Oscar Wilde

≈

Please don't talk when I'm interrupting.

Todd Rockefeller

≈

Happiness is nothing more than good health and a bad memory.

Albert Schwietzer

≈

If you have nothing good to say about anyone, come and sit by me.

Alice Roosevelt Longworth

≈

The trouble with high-tech is that you always end up using scissors.

David Hockney

It's true hard work never killed anyone, but I figure why take the chance?

Ronald Reagan

~

We joke because we don't know.

Anon

~

Whoever said money can't buy happiness didn't know where to shop.

Gittel Hudnick

~

Where there's a will, there are relations.

Michael Gill

~

It's not that I'm afraid to die, I just don't want to be there when it happens.

Woody Allen

Life would be infinitely happier if we could only be born at the age of eighty and gradually approach eighteen.

Mark Twain

≈

Life is just one damn thing after another.

Elbert Hubbard

≈

I don't want to achieve immortality through my work . . . I want to achieve it through not dying.

Woody Allen

≈

Death is the most convenient time to tax rich people.

David Lloyd George

Anyone can get old. All you have to do is live long enough.

Groucho Marx

~

I refused to attend his funeral. But I wrote a very nice letter explaining that I approved of it.

Mark Twain

~

On the plus side, death is one of the few things that can be done as easily lying down.

Woody Allen

~

I am prepared to meet my Maker. Whether my Maker is prepared for the ordeal of meeting me is another matter.

Winston Churchill

Millions long for immortality who don't know what to do on a rainy Sunday afternoon.

Susan Ertz

~

It's a funny old world – a man's lucky if he gets out of it alive.

W.C. Fields

~

There is no cure for birth or death save to enjoy the interval.

George Santayana

~

Retirement means twice as much husband and half as much money.

Anon

Smoking is one of the leading causes of statistics.

Fletcher Knebel

~

I don't need you to remind me of my age, I have a bladder to do that for me.

Stephen Fry

~

If you can't help out with a little money, at least give a sympathetic groan.

Jewish saying

~

A bank is a place that will lend you money if you can prove that you don't need it.

Bob Hope

Saving is a very fine thing. Especially when your parents have done it for you.

Winston Churchill

∾

Money is better than poverty, if only for financial reasons.

Woody Allen

∾

The two most beautiful words in the English language are "cheque enclosed".

Dorothy Parker

∾

The trouble with being poor is that it takes up all your time.

Willem de Kooning

I have long been of the opinion that if work were such a splendid thing the rich would have kept more of it for themselves.

Bruce Grocott

∽

The meek shall inherit the earth, but not the mineral rights.

John Paul Getty

∽

Whenever I feel the need for exercise I go and lie down for half an hour until the feeling passes.

Will Rogers

∽

We drink each other's health and spoil our own.

Jerome K. Jerome

He has no more patients because his patients are no more.

Lord Byron

~

All politics are based on the indifference of the majority.

James Reston

~

Democracy consists of choosing your dictators, after they've told you what you think it is you want to hear.

Alan Coren

~

A diplomat is a man who thinks twice before he says nothing.

Frederick Sawyer

Politicians are the same all over. They promise to build a bridge even when there's no river.

Nikita Khrushchev

≈

When I was a boy I was told that anyone could become president. I'm beginning to believe it.

Clarence Darrow

≈

Mr Attlee is a very modest man. But then he has much to be modest about.

Winston Churchill

≈

The Tory Party is the cream of society – thick, rich and full of clots.

Anon

A politician is a man who approaches every question with an open mouth.

George Canning

～

Happiness makes up in height what it lacks in length.

Robert Frost

～

It's far easier to forgive an enemy after you've got even with him.

Olin Miller

～

Intuition is reason in a hurry.

Holbrook Jackson

～

It is better to waste one's youth than to do nothing with it at all.

George Courteline

A speaker who does not strike oil in ten minutes should stop boring.

Louis Nizer

≈

The trouble with facts is that there are so many of them.

Samuel McChord Crothers

≈

Man is the only animal that blushes – or ought to.

Mark Twain

≈

I have a simple philosophy: fill what's empty, empty what's full and scratch where it itches.

Alice Roosevelt Longworth

If only we'd stop trying to be happy we could have a pretty good time.

Edith Wharton

~

The man who is a pessimist before forty-eight knows too much; the man who is an optimist after forty-eight knows too little.

Mark Twain

~

A psychologist once said that we know little about the conscience except that it is soluble in alcohol.

Thomas Blackburn

~

I shall lose no time in reading your book.

Benjamin Disraeli

I don't care what's written about me so long as it isn't true.

Dorothy Parker

≈

Once you've put one of his books down, you simply can't pick it up.

Mark Twain

≈

The covers of this book are too far apart.

Ambrose Bierce

≈

This is not a novel to be tossed aside lightly. It should be thrown with great force.

Dorothy Parker

Freedom of the press in Britain means the freedom to print such of the proprietor's prejudices as the advertisers don't object to.

Hannen Swaffer

~

Acting is merely the art of keeping a large group of people from coughing.

Ralph Richardson

~

The play was a great success, but the audience was a total failure.

Oscar Wilde

~

Nature has given women so much power that the law has wisely given them very little.

Samuel Johnson

As long as a woman can look ten years younger than her own daughter, she is perfectly satisfied.

Oscar Wilde

~

Is it possible that blondes also prefer gentlemen?

Mamie Van Doren

~

Whatever women do, they must do twice as well as men to be thought half as good. Luckily, this is not difficult.

Charlotte Whitton

~

The hardest task in a girl's life is to prove to a man that his intentions are serious.

Helen Rowland

A woman who strives to be like a man lacks ambition.

Anon

~

If a woman hasn't met the right man by the time she's twenty-four, she may be lucky.

Deborah Kerr

~

She is a peacock in everything but beauty.

Oscar Wilde

~

I used to be Snow White, but I drifted.

Mae West

~

High heels were invented by a woman who had been kissed on the forehead.

Christopher Morley

Women's styles may change but their designs remain the same.

Oscar Wilde

~

When women go wrong, men go right after them.

Mae West

~

Religion has done love a great service by making it a sin.

Anatole France

~

Behind every successful man stands a surprised mother-in-law.

Hubert Humphrey

Love: a temporary insanity curable by marriage.

Ambrose Bierce

~

If we take matrimony at its lowest, we regard it as a sort of friendship recognized by the police.

Robert Louis Stevenson

~

If parents would only realize how they bore their children.

George Bernard Shaw

~

If love is the answer, could you rephrase the question.

Lily Tomlin

~

Love is what happens to a man and woman who don't know each other.

W. Somerset Maugham

Happiness is having a large, loving, caring, close-knit family in another city.

George Burns

Bigamy is having one wife too many. Monogamy is the same.

Oscar Wilde

Men have a better time of it than women; for one thing they marry later; for another thing they die earlier.

H. L. Mencken

Insanity is hereditary. You get it from your children.

Sam Levenson

When I was fourteen, my father was so ignorant I could hardly stand to have him around. When I got to twenty-one, I was astonished at how much he had learned in seven years.

Mark Twain

❧

I haven't spoken to my wife in years — I didn't want to interrupt her.

Rodney Dangerfield

❧

Never lend your car to anyone to whom you have given birth.

Erma Bombeck

❧

Marriage is the alliance of two people, one of whom never remembers birthdays and the other never forgets them.

Ogden Nash

I like children. If they're properly cooked.

W.C. Fields

~

Children and zip fasteners do not respond to force . . .
Except occasionally.

Katharine Whitehorn

~

Luck is a matter of preparation meeting opportunity.

Oprah Winfrey

~

We must believe in luck. For how else can we explain
the success of those we don't like.

Jean Cocteau

~

Wickedness is a myth invented by good people to
account for the curious attractiveness of others.

Oscar Wilde

There are two times in a man's life when he should not speculate: when he can't afford it, and when he can.

Mark Twain

~

He who laughs, lasts.

Mary Pettibone Poole

~

I must decline your invitation owing to a subsequent invitation.

Oscar Wilde

~

If a scientist were to cut his ear off, no one would take it as a sign of heightened sensibility.

Peter Medawar

Duty is what one expects from others, it is not what one does oneself.

Oscar Wilde

Living with a saint is more gruelling than being one.

Robert Neville

∼

A conference is a gathering of important people who singly can do nothing, but together can decide that nothing can be done.

Fred Allen

∼

Saturday afternoon, although occurring at regular and well-foreseen intervals, always takes this railway by surprise.

W.S. Gilbert

∼

The worst part of having success is to try finding someone who is happy for you.

Bette Midler

We owe a lot to Thomas Edison – if it wasn't for him, we'd be watching television by candlelight.

Milton Berle

~

If all economists were laid end to end, they would not reach a conclusion.

George Bernard Shaw

~

The right to be heard does not include the right to be taken seriously.

Hubert Humphrey

~

Nothing needs so reforming as other people's habits.

Mark Twain

Any fool can tell the truth, but it requires a man of some sense to know how to lie well.

Samuel Butler

~

A lie can be halfway round the world before the truth has got its boots on.

James Callaghan

~

How come there's only one Monopolies Commission?

Nigel Rees

~

A door is what a dog is perpetually on the wrong side of.

Ogden Nash

If not actually disgruntled, he was far from being gruntled.

P.G. Woodhouse

~

Space isn't remote at all. It's only an hour's drive away if your car could go straight upwards.

Sir Fred Hoyle

~

A jury consists of twelve persons chosen to decide who has the better lawyer.

Robert Frost

~

It is better to keep your mouth shut and to appear stupid than to open it and remove all doubt.

Mark Twain

A celebrity is a person who works hard all his life to become well known, then wears dark glasses to avoid being recognized.

Fred Allen

~

Lots of folks confuse bad management with destiny.

Frank McKinney Hubbard

~

The fellow who laughs last may laugh best, but he gets the reputation of being very slow-witted.

Leo Rosten

~

God made Adam before Eve because he didn't want any advice on the matter.

Patrick Murray

Fred Astaire was great, but don't forget that Ginger Rogers did everything he did, backwards and in high heels.

Bob Thaves

❧

If only he'd wash his neck, I'd wring it.

Anon

❧

Women are more irritable than men, probably because men are more irritating.

Anon

❧

All men are of the same mould, but some are mouldier than others.

Anon

If you think women are the weaker sex, try pulling the blankets back to your side.

Stuart Turner

~

I married beneath me, all women do.

Nancy Astor

~

Always suspect any job men willingly vacate for women.

Jill Tweedie

~

Every other inch a gentleman.

Rebecca West

~

Not all men are annoying – some are dead.

Anon

If you think nobody cares whether you are alive or dead, try missing a couple of car payments.

Ann Landers

~

If you don't drink, smoke or drive a car, you're a tax evader.

Tom Foley

~

Hardware is the part of the computer that can be kicked.

Jeff Pesis

~

Please don't ask me to relax – it's only the tension that's holding me together.

Helen Murray

Conscience is the inner voice which warns us that somebody may be looking.

H.L. Mencken

∾

Several excuses are always less convincing than one.

Aldous Huxley

∾

As guests go, you wish he would.

Anon

∾

I never forget a face, but in your case I'll be glad to make an exception.

Groucho Marx

∾

Nothing is more responsible for the good old days than a bad memory.

Frank P. Adams

When there's nothing more to be said, he'll still be saying it.

Anon

~

Only dull people are brilliant at breakfast.

Oscar Wilde

~

I do not participate in any sport that has ambulances at the bottom of the hill.

Erma Bombeck

~

You're not drunk if you can lie on the floor without holding on.

Dean Martin

A woman drove me to drink and I never even had the courtesy to thank her.

W.C. Fields

~

An expert is one who knows more and more about less and less.

Anon

~

Don't let yesterday take up too much of today.

Will Rogers

~

Foolproof systems do not take into account the ingenuity of fools.

Gene Brown

Make three correct guesses consecutively and everyone will regard you as an expert.

Anon

≈

I started out with nothing and I've still got most of it left.

Anon

≈

Wrinkles merely indicate where smiles have been.

Mark Twain

≈

I'm at the age where my back goes out more than I do.

Phyllis Diller

≈

I have overcome my will-power and have taken up smoking again.

Mark Twain

She looks like a million dollars – after taxes.

Anon

~

If you get to be one hundred you've got it made – very few people die past that age.

George Burns

~

Most people who are as attractive, witty and intelligent as I am are usually conceited.

Joan Rivers

~

Dolphins are so intelligent that within only a few weeks they can train a man to throw fish at them from the side of a pool.

Anon

Eyewitnesses were on the scene in minutes.

Adam Boulton

~

This is the sort of English up with which I will not put.

Winston Churchill

~

The insurance man told me that I was covered for falling off the roof but not for hitting the ground.

Tommy Cooper

~

I love flying — I've been to almost as many places as my luggage.

Bob Hope

Researchers have already cast much darkness on this subject and if they continue their investigations we shall soon know nothing at all about it.

Mark Twain

～

There's a fine line between fishing and standing on the riverside looking like an idiot.

Anon

～

There aren't enough days in the weekend.

Anon

～

Just when you think tomorrow will never come, it's yesterday.

Anon

I would have given my right arm to have been a pianist.

Bobby Robson

~

I have my faults but being wrong isn't one of them.

Jimmy Hoffa

~

He'll regret it to his dying day, if ever he lives that long.

Frank Nugent

~

Anyone who goes to see a psychiatrist ought to have his head examined.

Samuel Goldwyn

~

I read part of it all the way through.

Samuel Goldwyn

A friend is someone who will help you move; a good friend is someone who will help you move a body.

Alexei Sayle

~

When the guy who made the first drawing board got it wrong, what did he go back to?

Steven Wright

~

Once, during Prohibition, I was forced to live for days on nothing but food and water.

W.C. Fields

~

The trouble with referees is that they just don't care which side wins.

Tom Canterbury

A politician will always be there when he needs you.

Ian Walsh